LIVING WATER
AND INDIAN BOWL

AN ANALYSIS OF CHRISTIAN FAILINGS
IN COMMUNICATING CHRIST TO HINDUS,
WITH SUGGESTIONS TOWARD IMPROVEMENTS

LIVING WATER
AND INDIAN BOWL

AN ANALYSIS OF CHRISTIAN FAILINGS
IN COMMUNICATING CHRIST TO HINDUS,
WITH SUGGESTIONS TOWARD IMPROVEMENTS

Dayanand Bharati

William Carey Library
Pasadena, California
www.WCLBooks.com

Published by the William Carey Library
P.O. Box 40129
Pasadena, CA 91114
www.WCLBooks.com

ISBN: 0-87808-611-0

Cover design: Rachel Snodderly

PRINTED IN THE UNITED STATES OF AMERICA

DEDICATED TO
THE BHAKTAS OF CHRIST
IN HINDU SOCIETY

CONTENTS

Land of Dharma

India is a land of many different religions. Hinduism is a way of life with many different belief systems. It is significant that the proper name for "Hinduism" is "Sanatana Dharma," or "the eternal way of life." You can have whatever beliefs you like, but you are expected to live out "dharma." Your religion is expected to participate in the values and customs and organization of the society.

For Westerners, it can be disconcerting that Dayanand Bharati in this book does not address many philosophical or theological issues. In this regard, Dayanand is very "Hindu" (in the cultural sense) in his outlook. The emphasis is not on orthodoxy but on orthopraxis. Dayanand's critique of Christianity is not that its teachings are heretical or false in India. His critique is that Christians do not follow dharma. They do not participate in the Indian way of life. For Westerners, these external matters can seem peripheral, but in the Indian context it's the way you live and act that matters, not what you believe.

Hindus respect any religious person. Even as a foreign missionary, I have always found a willingness by Hindus to give me the benefit of the doubt. They assume that I am a person of spiritual character. To that extent, they anticipate that I am participating in the dharma of the land. Any Christian pastor is generally welcomed into Hindu homes for prayer and teaching. If a Hindu finds you to be a person of character and propriety, it does not matter to him that much if you have differing theological beliefs. What matters first and foremost is that you are a person of dharma

I was speaking with an evangelist in South India about a new congregation that had been started in a slum area. At the dedication of the small worship facility, local Hindu and Muslim leaders were invited to address the crowd. He reported that they all praised the congregation and the work, even though converts had come from their own religions. They said they rejoiced that the congregation's ministry had brought more dharma into the community: order, respect, decorum. The bottom line is not what you believe but what you are.

Rejection of Dharma

It is argued that the Christians do not want to be part of dharma. The vast majority are from the "dalit" background, i.e., the untouchables and tribals. Even though they were counted among the Hindu population, they never felt a part of the religion. In fact, they strongly resented the Hindu way of life, for they were excluded and demeaned by it. Millions of dalits have become Christian precisely in protest against the dharmic way of life that had oppressed them for so many centuries.

At the time of the British colonization, when most of the conversions took place, becoming a Christian had a double payoff. On the one hand, it was an assertion of human dignity over against their Hindu persecutors. On the other hand, it was a move into the prestigious world and benefits of the Western powers in the land. The converts often got special treatment, including education opportunities, overseas travel, and employment from their Western co–religionists.

During the period of the mass conversions among the dalits, there was a popular opinion that Western civilization was more advanced than Indian civilization. By joining the Christian religion, dalits were not only rejecting an oppressive civilization but joining a higher one. In the South, there were enough numbers of converts that they could safely and conveniently remain in their villages. In the North, however, the numbers were fewer, so many converts moved into the towns and cities to become part of the Western mission life there.

These movements of socio–religious revolt against Hindus continue to this day. No longer is there any opinion that Western culture is superior, but there is strong opinion among dalits that the oppressive attitudes and practices of Hindu dharma will never change. This conviction continues to be the impetus for many conversions to Christianity, Islam, and Buddhism. These movements are highly political, for converts change their voting patterns and their social allegiances. They no longer accept the Hindu ideologies that they feel have kept them oppressed for so many centuries. They want justice now, not in some future life.

As dalits, Christian converts had no desire to be a part of the general culture, the dharma, of the nation. They resented and rejected it. Much of our Western view of the Indian caste system has been colored by the experience of dalit Christians. However, those 600 million who are in the caste system of India very much value it and enjoy it. They are embarrassed by the centuries–long oppression of the dalits and, since Independence, have generously effected "affirmative action" programs seeking to undo the suppression, at least economically.

Of course, the anger of the dalits remains, and we see it reflected in the "dalit theology" of today. Often this theology is full of vituperative and antagonistic analyses of dharma. Such attitudes certainly are understandable and to some extent relevant. However, it must be clear that such theology from India is not "Indian theology." It is the theology of the dalit church. It speaks to the 20% of the Indian population who are dalits. It does not speak to the 12% who are Muslim or the two–thirds who are in the castes.

India is a land of many different cultures and many different religions. Within Hinduism itself, one can identify hundreds of different religious traditions. Indigenous Christian theology grows out of the thought forms and quests of the culture. In the Indian context, there would then need to be hundreds of different theologies.

One of these indigenous theologies has begun to develop, the dalit theology. It has its legitimate place. The church with its westernized forms also has its place. The Christians are comfortable with its forms of worship and governance. They are Western forms, but that is why they were welcomed and now they are well rooted in the dalit church.

However, we must be clear that these forms and this theology do not speak to the vast majority of the land. The vast majority will never join the dalit church. We cannot expect the dalit church to have an effective outreach beyond its own dalit community. Certainly, as only 2.5% of the Indian population, the Indian church has plenty to do in evangelizing and serving their fellow dalits.

A Dharmic Theology

In this book, Dayanand Bharati does not propose to write an Indian theology. His role is more negative than positive, more iconoclastic than constructive. Dayanand attempts to show why the existing church in its structures and practices and thinking cannot relate to the two–thirds of India who are in the castes. In the Western world, it took centuries for a John of Damascus and an Origen and a Thomas Acquinas and a Martin Luther to arise. These great theologians arose from the culture and spoke to the culture, in very different ways. It may well take some centuries for their equivalents to arise on the Indian scene. In this book, Dayanand attempts to clear the path for such Indian greats yet to come.

In the past, this Christian voice that spoke to the general Hindu culture did arise in the Indian church. Generally, these were the voices of caste converts, who were attempting to relate their Christian faith to their own cultural identity. They needed to do this both for the sake of their own comfort in the faith and for the sake of conveying the faith to their fellow "Hindus."

However, we cannot realistically expect those voices to be heard in the church today.

As part of the social movement toward personal dignity among dalit Christians, dalit leaders have asserted that their agenda will be the agenda of the church. They will speak for the church, since they are the vast majority. The voice of the church will be a dalit voice. The leaders of the church will be fellow dalits. They did not leave Hindu dharma in order to once again fall under caste Hindu leaders and theologies. In Protestant churches, dalits want dalit pastors and they elect dalit leaders.

With this reality, the place of the caste Hindus in the church is problematic. It will be very difficult for a dharmic theology to develop. The soil isn't there to nurture and support it. The dharmic way of life simply is not the culture of the vast majority of Christians, whether in outcaste villages in the South or in mission cantonements in the North.

Culturally rooted dharmic theology will have to grow in different soil than that in the organized church of India. Dayanand Bharati's unique role has been to serve as a spiritual guide and interpreter for some of the "Jesu bhaktas" (devotees of Jesus) around the country. I don't know that anyone else has ever attempted this ministry in the history of Christian mission in India. Because Dayanand's voice is unique today and significant, we must give it special attention. If a theology that is rooted in dharma is to develop, it will have to develop outside the church. Dayanand is crucial in keeping that spark of possibility alive.

A Dharmic "Church"

However, in the Indian context, a dharmic Christian theology will remain secondary to the development of a dharmic Christian way of life. Western Christianity is always asking for and promoting theology as the life and sign of the church. My guess is that the historical emphasis, even to this day, on developing an Indian theology has much more to do with pleasing the Western church than to relating to the real interests of the Indian people. Our church leaders are trained in the West and trained to speak to the West, and our seminary curricula and content are modeled after Western interests. Our church theologians rejoice to please their Western audiences.

A truly dharmic theology will have to develop outside of these precedents and expectations. It will have to be a church significantly different from the organized church that we have now, largely populated and determined by dalits. It will have to be a church characterized much more by dharma than by theology.

Here is where our attention turns to the hundreds of thousands of Jesu bhaktas living outside the organized church. They need to be strengthened and guided in their lonely struggles to be faithful to our Lord. We can only hope and pray that many more Christian gurus like Dayanand Bharati will respond to God's Spirit. They won't come out of the formal seminaries, but out of the soil of the land, just as the great gurus of Hinduism do. They will need to arise in each of the hundreds of caste groups where Jesu bhaktas live and pray. These Jesu bhaktas need nurture not only to remain steadfast in the faith but to share it effectively among their families and communities.

Even though the Jesu bhaktas for the time being at least must remain separate from the church, they also sorely need the church. They can easily slip into heresy. They can easily compromise their faith and their witness. They can easily get exhausted by the struggle and meld back into the Hindu religious fold. At least until they have their own Christian gurus, they will need pastoral guidance and support. They need the affirmation and support of the organized church, though not its control and direction.

I hope that this book will motivate church people in India and around the world to appreciate the struggles of the Jesu bhaktas. They are the key to reaching the dharmic world of India. The Jesu bhaktas must be enabled to develop a church life that is rooted in dharmic soil where they live. This book should be a resource for all of those who even now reach into the lives of the 600 million people who live in India's caste system, through mass media, evangelistic conventions, pilgrimage centers, literature, Bible correspondence courses, etc.

Thanks to this book, we have a good idea of what we shouldn't do and some suggestions as to what we should do. Will we respect the dharmic culture of India, will we love the people of India's castes, will we value the courageous Jesu bhaktas, enough to change our ways? If we don't, we know we will be just as unsuccessful in our outreach to caste India in the future as we have been in the past. If we take the approach Dyanand Bharati proposes, the Gospel of our Lord Jesus Christ may flow smoothly and powerfully, with fewer unnecessary hindrances.

Can you imagine a church in India that draws on all the beauty and profundity of the ancient cultures of India? What a contribution that would be to the great nation of India and to the worldwide Christian fellowship. Let us join Dayanand Bharati in praying and working for that day.

Herbert Hoefer
Professor of Theology, Concordia University, Portland, Oregon, USA
Lutheran Church–Missouri Synod Mission Director for India and Sri Lanka
November, 2003

PREFACE

TO THE AMERICAN
REVISED EDITION

That this book was well received in some Christian circles, encouraged me to do a second Indian edition with some revisions. Most of the changes were additions of important quotes supporting the basic principles that had been outlined. But when I read Roland Allen's *Spontaneous Expansion of the Church,* I thought that I should have read it before writing *Living Water.* Maybe it is best that I did not since I would have extensively quoted from that book. In the end, I prepared a major synopsis of that book which appeared as an appendix to the second Indian edition. That has now been removed from this American edition as his book is better known and more accessible in the West.

A total re-editing of this book has been undertaken for this American edition, removing most of my idiomatic Indian English and convoluted sentence structure. I am very grateful to my friends, and particularly to Valerie Victoria, who did this tedious work.

Those who know little or nothing about life in India, which is family centered and society-based, may be confused by some of the principles and ideas which are suggested in this book. My aim is to form Christ-centered families within Hindu

(Indian) communities. All the suggestions given in this book center on this principle.

Understanding another society and community is not an easy process. When it comes to communicating the gospel, it becomes yet more complicated as we need to keep our commitment to biblical principles while at the same time being sensitive to the cultural and community values as well. In this process, as addressed in this book, many things have to be unlearned. We have always viewed things from our particular (cultural/social etc.) background, yet now must learn anthropological sensitivity on one hand and biblical faithfulness on the other. I hope that what is written here from the Indian context may help some in their "unlearning" process, before learning to communicate the gospel in any other context.

Dayanand Bharati
November 1, 2003

CHAPTER ONE

AN INTRODUCTION

Failure or inadequacy in communication is a common enemy to human happiness for it leaves the personality imprisoned. –James H. Jauncey, *Above Ourselves.*

The gospel of Jesus Christ is both a revelation as well as an initiation from God. The main reason for God to take the initiative to reveal His love for us is His concern for our salvation. So we, too, need the same concern in all our efforts to communicate the good news of Jesus to others.

"Communication" is not a one–way street. The very word itself denotes the involvement of another person who will respond to our efforts to communicate with him. But the tragedy is that, in spite of volumes and volumes of books on this subject (particularly in Christian teaching), in evangelistic endeavors among Hindus almost all efforts to communicate the gospel remain a one–way street.

Christians always seem to have a formula for "winning" (a militant and imperialistic term) Hindus for Christ, as if the Hindus have to blindly obey rather than to respond with a proper understanding of the gospel. The basic reason for such a wrong approach is that a uniform formula is imposed in the approach to any and every people group.

Of course, simple faith will cause one to follow Christ and a thorough understanding of theology and philosophy is not necessary. "For since in the wisdom of God the world through its wisdom did not know him, God was pleased through the foolishness of what was preached to save those who believe" (1 Cor. 1:21).[1] But we must make every sincere effort to present the basic tenants of the gospel, so that God can use that to reveal His grace to our listeners. Otherwise, all our labor to share the gospel becomes a waste. Let people deny Christ only after gaining a clear understanding of who God is and what they are before Him.

Since the beginning of this century, many conferences on evangelism developed evangelistic ideals often related with emotional slogans. These evangelical formulas may have been of some help to some people but largely ended up in voluminous writings that remain buried in the libraries. These are now only for research used only by those wanting to develop further slogans and formulas. At the popular level, of course, Christian slogans are painted on walls all across India, defacing property and embarrassing intelligent witnesses for Christ. Israel Selvanayagam relates an incident that shows the tragedy of such "witness":

> ...A few years ago through a special "evangelical campaign" in Madurai, the words "Jesus is the answer" appeared on the walls of Madurai town. The Hindus immediately responded by writing, "What is the question?" But there was hardly any Christian to acknowledge that Christians in this country have been trying to answer questions which have never been asked by the Hindus, while their real questions and the aspirations of the masses go unanswered....[2]

The solution to this communication problem lies not in raising emotional evangelical slogans like, "Within ten years, India will become a predominantly Christian country," nor in forming intellectual formulas in huge conferences on evangelism, but rather, we must begin by asking ourselves a few hard questions. If the question is asked, "Why is there no response among the Hindus, particularly among the so–called high caste people?" Then the answer to that question would be, "We are not properly reaching out to these people."

If the question is asked, "Why are people not confessing Christ?" The answer to that question would be, "There is no true communication about the Lord on our part." Moreover, the real challenge before us is to face these questions with thorough, factual and truthful answers.

What we need today is *practical evangelism,* not more slogans, conferences and theories. Those who take their vocation and call seriously to share the word of God must face the naked facts regarding *where we failed, why we failed and how we failed.* We must face heart–searching questions, especially, as they are raised by those whom we meet in our daily life as witnesses for Christ.

Where does the real problem lie in communicating the gospel to Hindus? First of all, we must understand that Indians do not want one more religion in the form of Western Christianity, which has largely lost its original meaning and become "Churchianity." Hinduism, alone, is called a parliament of religions.[3] Likewise, we do not need any more dogmas, creeds, codes of conduct, philosophies, etc. What we need is downright practical spirituality—*the living Christ* in His *original* form, as sent by God, lived by our Lord, witnessed by His disciples and promoted by His *bhaktas* (devotees) in the early centuries.

We must remember that religion should not be dogmas or denominational creeds but rather a *living spirituality.* It is much more an existence than an intellectual essence. Take an example from the Bible. Neither Jesus Christ nor His disciples preached any new dogma or philosophy to the people. They never spoke in absolute philosophical terms with a lot of metaphysical speculations (like we have in philosophical Hinduism, which always remained in the high altitude of human intellect),[4] nor did they give some new superstitions or blind–faiths such as are seen in popular (?) Hinduism and popular Christianity,[5] but they came to demonstrate practically how to live the God–given spirituality. They not only preached about spirituality, but also practiced it.

The Bible, as the word of God, is clearly not a philosophical book written to quench the intellectual urge of some people. Rather, it is a practical book and down–to–earth; we could

even say a work–manual, dealing with divine–human relationships. It is certainly not a book on religion, nor is it for the
private intellectual entertainment of a few individuals, but
rather, it is a book on relationships between God and man and
between men and men. Thus, we do not find any slogans or
formulas in it. Jesus and His disciples were uncompromising in
their teaching and practice, and what we need in India today is
the same uncompromising, practical spirituality, which Christ
demonstrated in his life.

This practical spirituality alone will help us to face all the
challenges confronting our Indian nation. "Show me that you
are saved, then I will believe in your Savior" is the challenge
before us.[6] But everywhere, we see a pathetic form of Christianity which is not ready to follow the command of Christ to "do
and preach" (Matt. 5:19).

Leaving aside the so–called "nominal Christians," even
those called "believers" are not following the footsteps of our
Lord who practiced and then preached. Christian leaders and
full–time workers want honor but without paying any price for
it. There is too much desire and expectation that our life standard should be raised, preferably to the level of a foreigner. The
longing to have an opportunity in the name of ministry to go
and visit the promised–land in the West, if not even to settle
there, remains among the unmentionable lusts that we try to
hide even from ourselves. The spirit of comparison is far too
much with us. But charity is not the monopoly of Christianity,
nor is renunciation the monopoly of Hinduism. The true spirit
of renunciation (which is not running away from responsibility
or "self–absorption" as some Christians cynically suggest) is the
correct antidote for present day materialism, which is present
everywhere, certainly not excepting Hindus.

If we, who wish to serve the Lord, want to face the challenges
of Hinduism, we must also deny ourselves, take up the cross,
and follow Him. But, as Zac Poonan has tragically pointed out,
"Whatever Christians may preach, when it comes to money,
everybody has the same religion." Prosperity theology and mate-

rialism, added along with casteism, power, position, division and authority are against the practical spirituality of Christ and the New Testament.

Before proceeding further, both as an answer and a challenge, let us see one practical solution to the question of why we have failed in our communication of the gospel. Personal concern must be the basic human attitude, which determines our communication. In other areas of life, people want to communicate because they want to express their aspirations, expecting others to cooperate with them. But in sharing the gospel, our concern must not be for our cause but rather solely concern for others–for their salvation. So we must think about the ways and means to communicate the gospel, being careful that in no sense do we either use people to satisfy our ego or act mainly to appease a guilty conscience (which many feel in light of the great commission (Matt. 28:19) and emotional appeals based on it). This principle is well stated in a British church document, "...The involvement of Christians in cultural and civic life ought to be motivated by love of neighbor, not by self–interest—not even by the corporate self–interest of the evangelical movement." [7]

If love is the only motive for us to worship and serve God, the same must also be our motive in serving others. But too much of our work in the ministry is done primarily as a duty, or else to fulfill some evangelical urge, which only shows our lack of true concern. By disposing such a duty, we are saying to the people, "Here is the message I have to give you (not to share with you) as I am under an obligation. Whether you understand it or not is not my concern." We see the genuine concern in the heart and mind of our Lord as well as His disciples to communicate the message to the people, and we too must have the same concern in communicating the gospel because *the gospel is never communicated until the message is understood.*

Leaving the secular world, where people mainly have concern to communicate to promote their products and get customers for them, in the religious world, we can see an example of this concern in the teachings of Swami Vivekananda. While he was in America teaching about monks (*sanyasis*) to his American disciples he said: "…If they (*sanyasis*) should eat of the tree of knowledge, they would become egoists and all the good they do would fly away.…Get rid of this puny 'I'; kill this diabolism in us. 'Not I, but thou'—say it, feel it, live it." [8]

See how he uses the words "tree of knowledge" and "not I, but thou" which his Christian disciples easily would understand. As Swamiji had concern for his disciples, he went down to their level to communicate his Neo–Vedantic ideas to them.[9] But Christians in India have yet to show the same kind of practical concern in communicating the gospel.

This book will bring to light, mainly by reference to incidents in my own experience, the present lack of practical concern in communicating the gospel to people of other faiths in India.[10] The main reason for sharing this is not to criticize or offend, but to share my heart's burden. I, too, could simply share a few formulas for evangelism, but that won't penetrate hearts and minds, which are immunized by such formulas. It is possible that some of my sharing might offend someone, but this cannot be helped. We cannot make an omelet unless we break the egg, and the purpose of this book is to break the egg.

Any criticism has its own limits, and without a solution no criticism holds any value in itself. The proposed solutions to the problems to be outlined below are not at all new, but rather just unpopular. Some ideas may seem new, as a new generation is not aware of all the discussions of the past.

In public expositions on this topic, especially to groups of missionaries and evangelical Christians, the end result has generally been in mere argument alone. Some reject these points even before an explanation is offered. This is primarily a reaction against Hinduism due to the belief that everything in Indian culture is pagan. Some listen attentively yet conclude by questioning why such a radical shift away from present traditions should be undertaken. The very few who finally understand the depth and reality of our need for change hesitate to take even a first step because of the fear of criticism from others within their circle, or perhaps because of the sheer amount of work it will entail to learn about the culture and religious faith of the Indian people.

This dismal and discouraging response helped me to understand further the depth of our problem. As most of the Christians in India are largely cut off from the rest of society, both culturally and socially, they cannot even understand how others view the gospel and Christianity. Missionaries are involved in *kabaddi* evangelism; once in a while they go out and touch the people, immediately returning back to their comfortable compounds or houses, having finished their evangelical duty.[11] They may live amidst Hindus but never will be deeply involved with their lives. Working on the mission field, it is as if they forget that there exists a society around them and are often involved in what Rev. John Stott rightly calls "evangelistic raids":

> Of course we make occasional evangelistic raids into enemy territory (that is our evangelical specialty); but then we withdraw again, across the moat, into our Christian castle (the security of our own evangelical fellowship), pull up the drawbridge, and even close our ears to the pleas of those who batter on the gate.[12]

Just ask any missionary whether they are ever involved in the cultural, social and religious life of the people among whom they live and serve. Even on popular public festival days like *Diwali, Holi, Pongal* and *Rakhi* (Rakshabandan) they will neither visit their neighbors' houses nor allow them to come to their houses. Whatever may be the religious connection behind these festivals, they are still vibrant social occasions that provide the best opportunities to mingle with and learn a lot about people. The great objection to any involvement is "what about the *prasad,* which they will give?" This specific issue will be addressed later, but we cannot afford to miss any opportunity to learn about the lives and needs of the people among whom we live and serve.

The worst tragedy is that not only will the Christian missionaries refuse to participate in any of their Hindu neighbors' festivals, but they will also discourage (if not forbid) Hindu "converts" from participating in their own family functions and common festivals even though socially (rather than religiously)

oriented. This they do to protect the new believers from the evil
influence of Hinduism. Dr. R. B. Rokhaya makes this point
from his experience in Nepal:

> Non—Christian festivals and rituals are only talked about in terms of
> temptation. During *Dasain* (*Dasera*), *Tihar* (*Diwali*) and national holidays,
> churches organize events in order to prevent people from going home and
> being tempted or forced to participate in the rituals. While Nepalis from all
> corners of the country and even from abroad travel home, Christians gather
> within the four safe walls of their churches. When people fail to abstain
> from rituals, for instance when they cut their hair or wear white clothes af-
> ter a family member has died, they are not allowed to enter the church.[13]

The same situation is present here in India also. "Win the
winnable while they are winnable," the popular modern mission
slogan, only added fuel to this fire. In their efforts to win the
winnable, no one bothered to ask the question why others remain
unwinnable. If we are satisfied in winning the winnable, we
will not go any further. And those involved in such "winning"
ministries do not seem to even want to pray for such additional
difficult tasks. Faithfully following the steps of their Western
predecessors, traditional evangelistic work goes on, of course,
with improved technical assistance. Most Christian workers still
faithfully follow their tradition alone without any originality.

Yet, many of the Western missionaries who served in India
not only read the Hindu scriptures to acquire first hand knowledge about Hinduism, but they even mingled with the people
to the extent of participating in their festivals and even visiting
Hindu temples. Ellis O. Shaw, the famous Scottish missionary who served in Tamil Nadu (particularly in Arkonam and
Chingleput) says:

> ...on one quiet afternoon I went in [the temple] for a look round. There
> were many other idols....Afternoon worship with the waving of the lights,
> offerings and *puja* took place with me among the small group of worship-
> pers, and that finished, the young priest came forward and made presents
> to the worshippers of flowers taken from the garlands round the idol's
> neck for them to put in their hair, or if men, to place behind the ears. There
> was also an opportunity for the worshipper to take a little sacred ash and
> with three fingers smear it on the forehead. To me also he offered courte-
> ously flowers and ash, and I, giving my small coin by way of boon for the
> priest, as courteously refused with hands raised in *namaskaram*....[14]

This and many similar examples must impact present practices. We must step forward to learn from others, particularly from our neighbors. It is imperative that at least the following ideas be tried for some time, and see the results in our ministry. Without this practical attempt, all criticisms and defenses will remain purely theoretical. Why not give a chance to new approaches? Many converts have come very far to understand and adopt traditional methods; can we not now take a few steps in line with their suggestions to reach people? At least give a try, and then if not convinced go back to your own tradition and methods.

Notes

1 All Scripture quotations are from the *New International Version,* unless otherwise indicated.

2 Selvanayagam, Israel, *The Dynamics of Hindu Traditions,* Asian Trading Corporation, Bangalore, 1996, pg. 128.

3 Barrett, David B., *World Christian Encyclopedia,* Oxford University Press, 1988, pg. v.

4 Cf. P. V. Kane's insightful criticism of intellectualized faith:

> The highest metaphysical standpoint can be realized by only a few. For millions of men, the empirical standpoint alone remains....The few highly philosophical men may say that what is real is the one Absolute, that all else in only an appearance of that Absolute. Common men may, however, complain that explanations offered by these philosophers do not satisfy them or are beyond them. (P. V. Kane, *History of Dharmasastra,* Bhandarkar Oriental Research Institute, Pune, 1990, vol. V. part. II, pp. 1508–09.)

5 In my opinion, the common division of Hinduism into "popular" and "philosophical" aspects is artificial, but accommodating to common understanding, particularly among Christian readers, the terms are used here. "Philosophical" Hindus have their own "popular" practices and "popular" Hindus have their own philosophy. This is helpfully explained by Edgerton:

> Later Hindu thought developed primarily out of the hieratic, Rig–Vedic religion; but it contains also quite a dash of lower, more popular beliefs. The separation of the two elements is by no means always easy. The truth seems to be that, the speculations out of which the later forms of thought developed, were carried on mainly by priests, adherents of the hieratic ritual religion. Almost all the intellectual leaders of the community belonged to the priestly class. But they were naturally – almost inevitably – influenced by the popular religion which surrounded them. Indeed, there was no opposition between the two types of religion, nor such a cleavage as our description may suggest. The followers of the hieratic cult also engaged in the practices that belonged to the more popular religion. This accounts for the constant infiltration from the "lower" sphere into the "higher," which we see going on at all periods. At times it is hard to decide whether a given new development is due to the intrusion of popular beliefs, or to internal evolution within the sphere of the priestly religion itself. (Franklin Edgerton, *The Bhagavad Gita Translated and Interpreted,* Mothilal Banarsidass Publishers Pvt. Ltd., Delhi, 1996 (1944), pg. 10.)

6 Dr. Radhakrishnan said to his missionary friend, "You Christians seem to us Hindus rather ordinary people making extraordinary claims." When the missionary explained that the claims were made on behalf of Christ, he observed, "If your Christ has not succeeded in making you better men and women, have we any reason to suppose that he would do more for us, if we became Christians." (from Selvanayagam, op. cit., pg. 132.)

7 *Seed of Hope: Report of a Survey on Combating Racism in the Dioceses of the Church of England,* by the Committee on Black Anglican Concerns, the General Synod of the Church of England, London, pg. 55.

8 Vivekananda, Swami, "Inspired Talks", *Selections from the Complete Works of Swami Vivekananda,* Advaita Ashram, Calcutta, 1986, pg. 394.

9 This "Neo–Vedanta", though claimed by several Hindu scholars like Dr. Radhakrishnan as another form of Sankara's Vedanta, is in fact very different from the orthodox Vedantic school. Rambachan in his excellent book clearly demonstrates this:

> [Sankara has] a radically different understanding of the nature and function of the sruti in relation to the gain of liberating knowledge. This understanding centered around Sankara's treatment of *sruti* as *sabda–pramaana,* a source of valid knowledge (*pramaana*) composed of

words (sabda). This view of the scripture, with all its implications, was in thorough and remarkable contrast to the status and function assigned to *sruti* in Vivekananda's representation of Advaita. The *sabda–pramaana* approach offered a very different rationale for the necessity of the scripture. (Anantanand Rambachan, *The Limits of Scripture: Vivekananda's Reinterpretation of the Vedas,* Sri Satguru Publications, Delhi, 1995, pp. 2–3.)

10   The word "non–Christian" is intentionally avoided as people should be called what they are (Hindus, Muslims, etc.) and not what they are not (non–Christians).

11   Readers unfamiliar with Indian culture may note that *kabaddi* is a game in which members of one team, while holding their breath, leave their safe area and try to touch members of the other team, running back to their side after exhausting their breath.

12   John Stott, *Issues Facing Christians Today,* Gospel Literature Service, Bombay, 1989, pg. 14.

13   "What if all Nepalis became Christians?" Dr. Rokhaya, R. B., *Face to Face,* Number 9, 1996, pg. 31.

14   Shaw, Ellis O., *Rural Hinduism: Some Observations and Experiences,* ed. A. P. Appasamy, CLS, Chennai, 1986, pg. 28.

CHAPTER TWO

CHRISTIAN FAILURE TO UNDERSTAND THE HINDU MIND AND CULTURE

Each person has his own way of thinking, understanding and approaching life. This is called his worldview. To present the gospel, we must have a proper understanding of peoples' worldviews related to culture, religion and society. Without having a proper understanding of the worldviews of the people among whom one serves, the gospel cannot be presented effectively. Particularly in India, where we cannot separate a Hindu's life into water tight compartments like cultural, social, religious, etc., not just a brief survey but a proper and deep study of their religion, society and culture is essential. Largely due to our Christian prejudices toward the religious, cultural and social life of Hindus, we have failed to study their worldview.

Convictions and Relationships

When we judge a person or thing, we always stand on the strong ground of our own personal convictions. Standing on firm convictions and making judgments cannot be considered wrong. However, our attitude and approach towards others are often not based on our conviction within us but rather on their relationship with us. The inner conviction that we should accept people as they are is too easily swept aside in reactions to others' relationships with us. If a person is friendly with us, then our relationship would be based on our reaction rather than on our conviction. If he is hostile, we will retreat.

This basic fact of human nature is a major stumbling block in building positive relationships with Hindu neighbors. Reaching your neighbor for Christ is an art. Rising above the normal human nature, we must try to reach them as God has reached us; which is through Christ accepting us as we are.

Understanding and Being Understood

To make our message understandable to our audience, we must have a proper understanding of their needs. Mostly, we simply assume that all ministry is successful and every message is well received. Particularly those who are involved in preaching live with an assumption that whatever they may preach people will understand. Yet most of the time, they preach not to the true need of the people but rather seemingly to their own satisfaction. This is not a problem unique to India, as the following illustration from an esteemed American missiologist shows:

> Several years ago, I was invited to speak in a newly planted congregation in an East African city. Both missionaries and nationals had been involved in the effort. Preceding the preaching service was a Sunday school with "classes for all ages." I joined the adult Bible class, which, for the size of the church, was amazingly small despite probable cultural factors militating against a large adult class. The missionary teacher was teaching the book of Romans. His outline, content, illustration and approach could as readily have been used in East St. Louis. He seemed oblivious to the fact that the entire lesson, and probably the choice of Romans itself, grew out of his upbringing, theological training and ministry experience in a culture far removed from Africa. When class members introduced themselves later, it became apparent that only those who were interested in Western culture (largely for professional reasons) had bothered to join the class. (That is discouraging because African believers desperately need biblical instruction that is relevant to their worldview!)[1]

Identical charades are acted out each week in India. Except for rare exceptions, most missionaries, and especially those who serve among Hindus (and emphatically here the reference is to Indian nationals, not primarily foreigners), know little about their peoples' culture and religious beliefs. It is supposed that some basic knowledge of the Bible is qualification enough for one to start working among Hindus. With little preparation and training, they straightaway enter ministry, carrying many prejudices along with them. For a typical evangelical missionary, everything in a non–Christian society, including its various cultural aspects, is from the devil. A Hindu is considered as a follower of Hindu religion, wherein he worships the devil in the form of several gods. They are idolaters, keeping cruel blind faith, which has with it a dreadful social evil called casteism, even including untouchability.

Wherever I have gone to teach among missionaries, I asked them to write a paper on "The Hinduism that I Know." And to my surprise, most of them wrote along the above lines. One Hindu convert even wrote that "Hinduism is a ZERO" (his own capitals); when I later asked him what made him write such words, he said, "This is what they (the Christians) say, so I wrote the same." So the same attitude of aversion that Christians grow up with is passed on to new believers. In order to remove such an aversion and many prejudices, we must have a proper understanding about Hinduism.[2]

The All Sufficiency of the Bible

Evangelical Christians always talk about the all sufficiency of the Bible, which is indeed a true doctrine when properly understood. On the other hand, one evangelical pastor in the north once said to me, "By reading all these books on Hinduism, you are wasting your time. All we need is to read the Bible properly and preach the gospel." He was not alone in this attitude. "When the early Protestant Tranquebar missionary, Ziegenbalg, sent home a thesis on Hindu beliefs and practices, his Halle professor told him 'not to waste his time with studying pagan nonsense'."[3]

> Almost two hundred years ago, the Serampore Trio (Carey, Marshman, and Ward) were misunderstood because of their efforts to understand the culture and religion of India. In fact, they devoted so much attention to this that some of their supporters back in England accusingly reminded them that they had been sent to convert the heathen, not to be converted by them! But those gifted and intrepid missionaries knew precisely what they were doing....And that is what he and his colleagues

were about –learning about India in order to adapt the presentation of the Biblical gospel most effectively.[4]

The Bible is certainly all–sufficient for understanding the truth of salvation. Yet, the Bible itself shows us that it is not to be the prime contact point with the world outside of Christ. In the synagogues, the world where at least to some extent Christ was known, the apostles preached from the Bible (Old Testament); in Athens, where Christ and the Bible were unknown, Paul did not use the Bible but began with general human understanding and the teachings of the Greek poets (Acts 17). So, true belief in an all–sufficient Bible will cause us to begin where people are and bridge to the Bible.

Anthropological Study

The study of anthropology (thankfully at least attempted by most mission societies) should not be limited to the training period but must be continued on the mission field. To my surprise, I found that most missionaries do not understand or even recognize the simplest social customs observed among Hindus in north India. Once, in conversation with a missionary, I realized that he did not even know that women born in a village, even after their marriage, need not cover their heads when they visit their parents; but only women who come to the village from outside, as the wives of the men of that village, have to cover their heads. This is to recognize who are the daughters of the village and who are daughters–in–law. Such a practice is not present in south India, and being a south Indian, he failed to observe cultural aspects in his mission field in the north.

Until we know the social customs of the people, we cannot work out proper strategies to reach them and we may even use wrong methods, which may finally close that very society for the gospel. I once heard that two students from Union Biblical Seminary, out of over zealousness to preach the gospel, discontinued their study and went to a tribal community in Andhra Pradesh. Soon after they started the work, without having proper understanding of the local social customs, they compelled new believers to remove their bangles. That was enough for the ministry to be closed. Instead of sharing the gospel, the main message communicated was that they went there to break the bangles of the women.

An example of sensitivity to social (and even religious) customs and the use of them as a means to convey the truth and bring success can be given from the famous story of Bruchko, Bruce Olson and his ministry among the Motilone tribes in Colombia, South America. He wrote:

> In a few years, there were eight health stations that gave shots, antibiotics, and other medicines. These also were in charge of seeing that the Motilone homes were kept free from germs. Each home developed its own agricultural system as well, and eventually schools were established.
>
> The health centers, the farms, and the schools were not set up or staffed by civilized white people. They were staffed by the primitive Motilone Indians. I was the only outsider in the Motilone area....
>
> It is considered by many to be the fastest example of development that has ever occurred in a primitive tribe. How did it happen? How was this possible?
>
> There are two reasons. The first is simple: The Motilones were not asked to give up their own culture and become white men. Everything introduced was built on things they already knew. Vaccination, for instance, was introduced by the witch doctor as a new form of the traditional blood—letting, that the Motilones practiced when someone was sick because, like blood—letting, it gave a pain that overcame the greater pain of disease or death. Explained in that way, and administered by the witch doctor, who was known and trusted, it quickly was accepted and spread through the tribe.... The second was the Holy Spirit...[5]

In the communication of the gospel of Christ, it must be spoken in the language of the people, whether it is mythical, metaphysical or secular.[6] Otherwise, those who accept the gospel or reject it will not do so with an understanding of what they accept or reject. From Madagascar, Dr. Merle Davis illustrates the problem of communication in its relation to existing patterns of understanding:

> In Madagascar, after a generation of proclaiming Jesus as the Lamb of God who sits on the right of His throne and whose blood alone can save from sin, the old chief of a tribe which had resisted the Christian message revealed the reason for his peoples' indifference. "We are a cattle—raising people; we despise sheep. Our clans asked the early missionaries whether there was a place on God's throne for a cow as well as a sheep, and when they were told "no," they closed their hearts to the Christian gospel.[7]

Without first observing and studying the culture of a particular community, we should not even dare to start the ministry. About their religious worldviews, we may collect some second hand information by reading books, but regarding the culture, we must learn first hand by careful observation before beginning the actual work of the ministry.

Dangers in the Missionary's Teaching Role

It is generally believed that, "New believers are just babes, and they don't know which aspect of their culture is biblical and which aspect is not. Therefore, it is our responsibility to teach them thoroughly on these issues." I too, agree with this. But before we *dare* to teach them, we must have a firm grasp of the essentials of their worldview. Bruce Olson provides another striking illustration:

> Some parables didn't seem to fit the Motilone culture, either. Take, for example, the parable of the man who built his house on rock so that it would be firm. When Bobby first heard it, he suggested that it be deleted. "That's not right, Bruchko. A house that is solid must be built on sand. Otherwise the poles won't go deep enough and the house will fall apart." So we adjusted the parable. After all, Jesus had chosen it to clarify a truth for his listeners. Wouldn't he want the Motilones to understand also?[8]

A Christian worker who is born and brought up in a culture other than the one he is working in will have his own prejudices against other cultures. Therefore, all his judgments of the cultures will be based on these prejudices. So first of all, he must recognize his own Christian (and human) prejudices against other cultures and try to incarnate himself completely in the new culture where he wants to serve and witness. As Michael Griffiths puts it:

> The Christian missionary has to make a deliberate, conscious and sustained effort to live and work and think and speak in the framework of that culture....We need to make vigorous efforts in changing cultures to adapt ourselves to presenting the unchanging gospel in terms of the changing environment. One questions the necessity of using 17th century language, 18th century hymns and 19th century evangelistic methods to reach 20th century man....Generally considerable adaptation is advisable. Otherwise your missionary is like a spaceman coming out of his hermetically sealed alien capsule....[9]

This is where the Western missionaries failed. Instead of adapting and adopting themselves to Indian culture, they not only preserved their own but also encouraged their converts to adopt that alien culture. There were few a exceptions like Fr. Robert de Nobili, S.J., and his friend Fr. Antonio Vico, S.J., but their efforts and methods to adapt to Indian culture were suppressed.[10] At the same time, as all novel things have their own attraction, the converts also quickly (generally too voluntarily) adopted Western cultural practices. This helped the missionaries to feel at home with their converts, but closed the rest of the society to the gospel:

> When the Portuguese came to India, they wanted to make people not only Christians; they wanted to make them Portuguese. They gave to converts not only Portuguese names and dress but also induced them to eat beef and pork and to drink liquor. In this way, they separated Christians as much as possible from the Hindu community to whom eating beef and drinking liquor was an abomination. Thus, it came about that in Goa and in many other places, Christians and Hindus formed two different communities, communities with different social customs.[11]

The following story, from the Madurai Mission during the time of Robert de Nobili, will help us to understand this fact. On the arrival of Nobili to Madurai on November 15, 1606, Fr. Goncalo Fernandez, S.J., was there—running a school and public hospital, yet without any evangelistic success, not even making a single convert during the fourteen years of his service there. All his zeal to preach the gospel was looked on by the populace of Madurai as an effort to convert them as "Paranghis." Why? In the words of Sauliere:

> But who were Paranghis? The word was the South Indian version of Feringhee, a term by which, since the time of the Crusades, the Muslims described the Franks or Westerners. The Portuguese had naturally inherited that name, and whatever was connected with them, their manner of living, their character, their religion, their culture, was summed up in the name Paranghi.[12] Anyone going about in trousers and wearing a coat and a hat, whether born on the banks of the Tagus or on the backwaters of Travancore, was a Paranghi. Paranghism became, in the eyes of Hindus, the refuge of criminals who had fallen foul of the laws of their country, of social rebels who sought to shake off the discipline of caste and the Hindu rules of decency. The Portuguese were well aware of the opprobrium attached to that name, but far from resenting it, they welcomed it

as a means of swelling their ranks and strengthening their hold on their followers. They would not trust the sincerity of their converts unless it was guaranteed by a participation in their banquets, loss of caste, change of name and dress, and the adopting of Portuguese customs. Once a man had become a Paranghi, he was irretrievably compromised in the eyes of his own people; he was looked upon as a traitor, ostracized and castaway; he had no choice but to cling to the Portuguese.[13]

Though we can neither blame the Portuguese for the wrong interpretation of their religion and culture by the local people nor the people for their lack of clear understanding of the cultural aspects separated from faith, yet Fr. Fernandez's own failure of promoting Paranghism at the cost of personal faith in Christ is the main reason for that deadlock:

Father Goncalo Fernandez was perfectly certain that no name was more glorious than that of Paranghi and he used it, without the least qualm of conscience, to describe his religion. He would, in his most ingratiating way, invite high caste Hindus to adopt the Paranghi religion, and when his invitations were met with contempt, he could find no other explanation than the ignorance of those poor people who could not appreciate what was good for them. Indian customs and Indian ways were to him nothing but a bundle of superstitions, which were to be carefully avoided. To suggest that they could go very well with a sincere profession of Christianity sounded blasphemous to him. The more his disciples discarded their ancestral customs, and the closer they adhered to Portuguese ways, the better Christians they would be. Paranghism, to him, meant Christianity, and he held that none could enter the latter unless he bore the authentic hallmark of the former. It never occurred to him that what his hearers rejected was not Christianity but the hated Paranghi customs with which it was identified; that he never realized this was his life's great tragedy. As a pioneer of the faith among the Badagas he had proved an unqualified failure.[14]

And in this process, the Protestant missionaries were no way better than the Roman Catholics. They too, for one reason or the other, separated the new converts from the rest of society by creating separate "Christian" colonies and villages. They thought that Christians in India should have a separate social identity (which is completely unbiblical), and for this, they encouraged the Christians to copy them, thinking that it will help the Indian Christians to keep a separate identity. And in this also, as Manilal Parekh rightly pointed out, "the so–called 'Indian Christian churches' form a community among other Indian communities and 'not a church' transcending them." [15]

This same mistake should not continue to be made today in the name of "teaching the new babes in Christ." Then first learn to remove your Christian prejudices before you dare to teach.

Here we have to note (not to hurt any community, but to see the truth) that at present in India, also, instead of its biblical and historical meaning, somehow the word "Christian" has a meaning not unlike "Paranghi" in Nobili's time. To join a church or become Christian means (at least to the so called high caste people) something social, just the same as it was to become "Paranghi" at Madurai. Excepting a few places, each denomination has a particular caste status and joining the church means becoming a member of another community. About this Hoefer says, "The correct description of the religious reality, at least in Madras City, is not that Christianity is a Harijan religion but a Harijan Church." [16] He points out that "Our Gurukul Director Rev. Gnanabaranam Johnson tells the story of one time when he asked a Nadar Christian student of his whether he would prefer a non–Christian Nadar wife or a non–Nadar Christian wife. He reports that the boy replied immediately, 'A Nadar wife, of course.'" [17]

When I have pointed out this fact that Christianity is only another community among many Indian communities rather than being a church which transcends all communities, several times I have been told that one should not blame either the church or the Christians for this as it is a problem of India (because of Hinduism which is based on caste), and so is not the particular fault of Christianity in India. It is easy to blame outsiders to justify your shortcomings inside the church or Christian community. If the Christians think that based on "neither Greek nor Jews" (Gal. 3:28) theory that the Bible expects them to form one uniform community without any differences, then they have to do it based on the authority of the Scripture and their commitment to Christ, and they should not blame the society outside for their shortcomings.[18] And above all, even in this so called Christian Community in India, there are different caste based communities (as the student wanted only

a "Nadar wife") and not one uniform community. Of course
the pro–Dalit group, keeping in mind the needs of the majority of Christians coming from that community, fight for their
rights. But several non–Dalit Christians say, "Why is there only
a Dalit theology and movement in the church? What about
those of us who are not Dalits? Why can there not be an OBC
(Other Backward Community) theology and movement also to
cater to our needs? Will a Hindu Nadar accept being branded
as a 'Dalit'?" This I share not to create any strife among the
various Christian caste–based communities in India, but only
to point out the reality.

Learning before Preaching

The greatest temptation in a missionary's life may well be to
start preaching immediately. Michael Griffiths calls attention to
this problem:

> When you get to your field of work, remember that learning that lan-
> guage is basic to your future usefulness. Pressures will be brought upon
> you to start doing this and that. You yourself will be eager to start preach-
> ing. But remember that there is little point in preaching your heart out, if
> it does not get into the heart of the other fellows. You can make noises,
> and use words, but if the net result is incomprehensibility, you have made
> no contribution to that person's salvation however much satisfaction you
> may kid yourself you are getting.[19]

This truth is applicable not only for language learning but
for all that we shared above. Time must be given for attending
the Hindu satsanghs, melas and marriages, as well as for reading
their scriptures and folk songs and collecting their proverbs, etc.
But the tragedy is that a pattern has been established of entering the field after one year of "urgent" training without even
properly knowing the language, and soon after arrival, taking a
bundle of literature to begin "business." All such "trainees" will
ever learn is some basic spoken language, which will be used in
the pattern of talk–talk–talk, with hardly ever any listening to
the people. That is why, in spite of their hard work, few get satis-
factory results in ministry.

Instead, first learn by collecting information. Even on those
points on which you cannot agree or understand, listen pa-

tiently. Then later, do not force your own ideas or give your own interpretation on any aspects of a new believer's or interested contact's life. Give them proper, appropriate and systematic Bible teaching, and allow them to decide for themselves on any crucial and delicate issues.[20] In the case of contacts, do not pressure them to "accept" Jesus Christ in your terms, but allow them to make their own decisions. They may go wrong initially, but if they do make mistakes, we can correct them gently by pointing it out under the light of the Scripture. Whereas, any hasty judgment or conclusion from your side may create serious damage to the ministry. Remember those UBS student's hasty action of breaking the bangles. *One quick step in the wrong direction, then we have to invest all our life to correct it.*

In an unpublished manuscript, I have seen one evangelical leader write that the pastor or evangelist must make a serious study of the culture and draw his own demarcation lines for a particular culture. Rather than solving the problem, this *is* the problem. However much an evangelist or pastor may study another culture, as he can never be a part of the other community, he cannot and should not "draw his own demarcation lines" in the name of guiding the new group. If the evangelist or pastor is a convert from this particular community and is now leading and evangelizing, he should be encouraged to study his own culture and to think through the Biblical implications of his culture's particular aspects, and then form his own demarcations (without any "brainwashing" by the missionary). He may go wrong initially, as he attempts to study his own culture (worldviews) "objectively." But let him make mistakes, which can be corrected gently rather than doing permanent damage for the furtherance of the gospel in the name of teaching the new believers.

A word must also be added about making a "serious study" of cultures. The same manuscript mentioned above states that action in accordance with culture is generally at the subconscious level. This is true and raises serious questions about "objective" studies of culture. Most of the written materials available for "objective" studies are done by outsiders. Outside experts can

give technical terms and precise scientific (anthropological) definitions about a culture, which are very helpful to comprehend
the subject under study. Some subjective involvement in a culture and community alone qualifies one for serious study about
a culture, but in the final analysis, the outsider (missionary in
our case) must recognize his limitations. Regarding the native,
his new faith in Christ or the prejudice of the missionaries towards his worldviews should not hinder his study about his own
culture. He must be given freedom to draw his own conclusions
about his culture from his experiences and his objective studies.
When he seeks help, the outside missionary can only help to the
extent that Bruce Olson did when his advice was sought regarding fighting against encroachers on tribal land (see note 20).

Vision
One main reason for lack of proper knowledge about the people
among whom the missionaries serve is lack of focused vision. Too
many go to a particular mission field because the organization
has sent them there. They do the ministry in the exact way as
their seniors are doing. They keep targets and goals because they
are decided in the planning meetings. But personally, they are
not doing the ministry because they have a vision in them for the
people. A missionary must be a visionary first. Otherwise, he may
spend all of his life in the Lord's work without properly investing
it: "A vision without a task makes a visionary. A task without a
vision is drudgery. A vision with a task makes a missionary."[21]

True Learning
"To learn" has now tragically become related to obtaining some
theological degree, and that, too often, just for the sake of the
certificate. Finish theology (that too, Western theology) in a
seminary or institute and enter the field and forget everything.
"Theological study in India won't give much help for missionaries to reach Hindus," said Dr. Roger Hedlund in a Bangalore
conference during January, 1991. Theological graduates serving
in evangelical circles do not seem to use what they have learned.
One of my friends who holds a Bachelor of Divinity degree was

asking a few questions to clear his doubts about me. I referred to a few books and used terms that I thought might be meaningful for him. "Yes," he said, "we heard about such terms and books while we were studying." Permit me to quote the words of one missionary from the mission field as an example:

> Tracing the changes in my own attitudes over the past 3 or 4 years, I can discern a definite shift for the better from a rigid stereotype mind set.... Much of my own reflections pertain to questions and issues that people here raise in the course of my ministry. We often give stereotype answers programmed into us without a proper appreciation of their perspectives, owing to which our answers and interactions fail to touch the heart of the issue. Though our emphasis on strategies and approaches ought not to detract us from our dependence on God's working on the one hand, complacency is as serious a lapse on the other. I do strongly feel that something ought to be done in the area of missionary training as well. The training given does not seem to make them fit for the field. It does not enable the adoption of proper attitudes on the part of the missionary, nor does it train his mind to evolve situation related approaches. The training at B.B.I. etc. seems to only run in more information without training the mind and hearts. Hope our leaders will address themselves to this need in future.[22]

Generally the regular program on a mission field is—go out—meet lots of people—distribute a lot of literature—conduct night meetings—share what you know (not what they need)—then send reports and be satisfied.

In my many years of involvement in Indian missions, I have never seen, in even a single field, "learning" (observing and collecting information) as one of the strategies to reach the people (of course there may be exceptions which I did not notice). Even if only half an hour a day is spent in observing and collecting information, a lot can be learned about the people. But, again recognizing rare exceptions, most missionaries never take a personal interest to be involved in learning about the culture and people.

Having their new faith on one side and living and facing lots of problems and challenges in their society, the life of every new convert becomes a *struggle for existence*. And to help them in their struggle, we must learn before we dare to teach anything to them.

The Mindset of the New Convert

We must also remember that an average Hindu knows little about his scriptural teachings and sanctions. Like an average Christian, who does not know everything about the Bible, an average Hindu is brought up faithfully keeping his traditions. According to Hinduism, faithfully keeping all the traditions of his own society is also a part of his religious duty (*dharma*), whether he agrees with them or not or understands them or not.[23] All he knows about his religion is traditionally handed over to him, often without his having any personal first hand knowledge. Furthermore, most new converts from Hinduism do not know whether any particular custom is cultural, social or religious. Taking such people's words seriously and as final on any issue may hinder our work.

Almost all new believers (with rare exceptions), because of over enthusiasm, overly criticize their own past religious faith, including cultural and social aspects. A Hindu convert will start to see that everything in his Hindu society is wrong and everything in his new–found faith with its Western *masalas* (spices) in Christian society is not only right but marvelous. After several years of experience, he will realize that he was wrong in his judgment on both sides. But now, to accept that he has made some mistakes in his judgment of both sides becomes a prestige issue for him. As in the case of some converts from the so–called high castes who in the meantime marry a Christian girl, they cannot possibly come out from the new "Christian" culture (and most of the time people will adopt any new culture more quickly than preserving an old one). This new culture may even embarrass him, particularly before his unconverted relatives. So in order to keep his prestige, he would rather go to the other side than come back to his original home situation with open recognition of his mistakes.

Take a new, born–again Christian from the traditional Christian background. Suddenly, he will see that all the activities of the other Christians, who according to him are nominal Christians, are totally unbiblical, and he will become extremely critical of them. Often, those who become Charismatic, born–again believers behave worse than a new believer from a Hindu background in the area of fault finding in his old church and society.

Therefore, we must be careful in learning from a new believer. The best way to learn about the cultural, religious and social habits of a given society is to learn from the society itself. First, enforcing a minimum period of one year of study in the field about all aspects of the peoples' life before starting into any ministry would prove a very fruitful policy in terms of long–term effectiveness. Also, a reinforcement of this study would be for the missionary to write a paper on what he has learned during that year.

Lack of Originality

Lack of originality and satisfaction in what is being done at present are important reasons for our failures. It seems that everything thought, said and done must be endorsed either by a Western scholar or Westernized Indian scholar. Otherwise, your idea will be rejected.

In the way of answering a few questions asked by a contact (to another missionary, the questions having been sent on to me), I prepared a paper on "Body, Soul and Spirit." Though I referred to several Bible verses, yet due to my complete lack of knowledge of both Hebrew and Greek, and as I could not get proper Bible dictionaries and other needed books to refer to at that time, I could not do full justice to the subject in that paper. However, my answer was in line with what we Indians (Hindus) understand and how we approach the subject (as the question was asked by a Hindu, not a Christian who might understand "Christian" terms). Though I used both Gita and Upanishads to explain the subject under discussion, I concluded the paper based on my personal understanding and experience in this matter.

Later, when I was teaching Hinduism to a group of missionaries, I shared that paper with them. One senior missionary, after pointing out a few fundamental unbiblical points (which I had failed to notice, but accepted immediately when shown), said: "If you could refer and use some of the Biblical scholarly books and also present what is the Bible's view about the subject, then alone your paper holds some weight. You often showed how Indian philosophical systems treated and approached the subject, but failed to bring the Bible's views regarding this subject."

Though I accepted his criticism to some extent, I humbly pointed out two facts: first, I did not altogether neglect what the Bible said about the subject. I both referred and explained what the Bible said, of course based on my understanding alone, as I could not refer to the scholars' views at that time. Second, even in the Bible one cannot come to a proper understanding (particularly on this subject of body, soul and spirit) as biblical theology, even in its formation stage, was influenced by other philosophical systems, like the Greek, etc.[24] Of course, I do not justify my mistake or limitation for not giving the whole biblical concept about the subject.

After several months, when again I started to think about the subject, I referred to as many scholarly works as I could get, and to my surprise, after reading them, I came to the conclusion that it would be irrelevant for us to try to teach any Indian believer (or seeker) any subject using terms and theology (borrowing from Greek and German) which he could never understand. An Indian can understand our biblical teaching only when we use the terms and systems for which he has some access and understanding. This does not mean that the biblical terms and systems are irrelevant with their Greek and Hebrew terms and philosophies. If we closely follow, we can clearly see how the apostles freely borrowed from the surrounding cultures and used entirely "pagan" terms and systems to convey the Old Testament teachings to the Gentile converts. The Gentiles could never have understood the Old Testament teachings if they came in uncommunicative terms.

But in Indian Christian circles, there is a strong feeling and influence that only if we use the exact terms and systems of Hebrew and Greek to convey any Biblical truth, then alone it is relevant. They seem least bothered about whether the person to whom we present the truth understands it or not. They will spend all their energy to pull him up to the level of their own understanding rather than going to his level to teach. Please note that this going down to his level does not mean that we have to compromise Biblical truth with his faith.

I cannot understand the desire of some Christians, that too particularly new converts, to learn Greek and Hebrew with much difficulty and pain in the name of understanding the Bible in its original form. Biblical Greek and Hebrew are difficult languages, which will demand a lot of time even to pick up some basic lessons to understand the Bible. Even if one becomes a master in those languages, what is the use of them where simple books are available in English to understand the Hebrew and Greek? This does not mean that none should spend time with Greek and Hebrew. Scholars in those fields will always be welcome, but an average disciple of Christ need not invest his precious time on such hard fields. Instead, if he tries to learn some basic Sanskrit and the scriptures of the land and the language of the people among whom he works, more work can be done successfully in ministry.

Culture and Truth

God used both the Jewish culture and religious system to reveal His truth to humanity. And His apostles used the Greek philosophy and terms to convey the same message to the Gentiles. Now to present the same truth to Indians, we should use the Indian framework and not that of Hebrew and Greek, nor Western. Dr. Radhakrishnan said that perhaps Christianity, which arose out of an Eastern background and early in its career got wedded to Graeco–Roman culture, may find her rebirth today in the heritage of India.[25] And in another place, he specifically suggested that "Students of Christian religion and theology, especially those who wish to make Indian Christian thought not merely 'geographically' but 'organically' Indian, should understand their great heritage which is contained in the Upanishads." [26]

We should never deviate from the fundamental teachings of the Bible. And in our efforts to convey the truth within an

Indian framework, if we sense the danger of syncretism, then we must give up the framework or rather adjust it to fit to that truth.

This adjustment doesn't mean that we can abuse or misuse the Hindu frame to make it fit our need. A sensitive handling of Hindu values and traditions is essential, and nothing should be done to hurt anyone's feelings and sentiments. For example, see appendix two on OM. However, not only are we not ready for this, but we are even ashamed of an attempt to use our own original frame in communicating any biblical teachings.

"Adjusting" the Indian philosophical framework is also a challenging concept; it does not mean that we can misuse Hindu philosophical and religious terms by ignoring their original contexts and completely redefining them for our purposes. Take for example *advaita* (non–dualism). No doubt, the various *advaitin* categories could serve as a framework to prepare an Indian Christian theology (as numerous Christian scholars have maintained and experimented with),[27] but we must be conscious of the danger of abusing the same *advaita* to use it for our purposes. Francis Clooney, S.J., warns of this danger: "*Advaita* has suffered at the hands of readers who have discussed its themes without sufficient attention to the manner in which these are inscribed in the Text." [28] This is a vast and difficult subject with dangers on every side, and these brief comments have not even begun a valid discussion. See some further discussion below in chapter 3 part D, "In Our Theology."

Originality

When I sent a small article called "Inculturalization" to one magazine, the concerned person replied, "You simply shared what you think based on your experience. But you must also quote what other scholars think and have done in the same area with some case studies. Then alone your paper will have some weight in any circle." "Do not have originality, but live like a parasite and always borrow your ideas from others," seems to be the meaning of that.

If a new convert struggles to pick up "Christian" traditions and practices, including jargon and manners, then he will be encouraged to press forward with much "faith." "In the beginning you won't understand these as you are just a baby in the Lord. Follow us, then one day you will even lead us," they will say. But it is all without any originality. Like the Pharisees of old, these Christians impose on new believers the traditions they have borrowed from others.

I was a victim of this, as one example demonstrates. We Indians are accustomed to addressing God only in familiar singular forms (*avan* in Tamil and *tum* in Hindi), as Westerners would use a first name. This is because, as a *bhakta* (devotee) comes close to his Lord, he forgets all formalities. But Christians in India (particularly Tamilians), observe many formalities in their dealings with the Lord. So following their steps faithfully, in the early days, I composed songs always using formal plural forms in addressing my Lord. But I never felt at home in those songs whenever I used them in my personal worship. Later when I realized my mistake of blindly accepting others' views, I not only composed in the natural way using familiar singular forms, but I also used the same in my personal prayers.

Unteachability

Ignorance can be excused, but unwillingness to learn is wrong in every way. Unteachability is the greatest crime. Particularly those who worship mere tradition are the most unteachable. As R. de Smet, S.J., has said, "Men are naturally conservative" [29] and they will not accept any change immediately. People prefer to feel secure in their present condition in which they live rather than venturing into new, unknown areas. And those who always venture for new experiences with much adventurous spirit, face opposition as people see in them a threat to their present security. We may preach from Acts 18:24–28, but to have the spirit of Apollos is quite another thing.

For example, in *satsangh* ministry, when I introduced the Sanskrit word *tatastu* in place of "amen," it was immediately welcomed by the new believers in Hindi speaking areas. But while most of the missionaries may half–heartedly permit the new believers to use the word, they will never utter it themselves. Even one senior missionary said, 'We are conservatives, and we won't accept changes." Another missionary whom I met three months after my visit to his field said, "The converts were saying *tatastu* only when you were there. After you had left, we won them back, and now they are again using 'amen'." This he said with a spirit of achievement because he does not want to learn from others. Naturally following his footsteps, the converts themselves eventually become unteachable. The spirit of Apollos must come to Christians in India!

One main reason for the lack of teachability is that the missionaries never step into the shoes of the new believers who have to face the problems. New believers, particularly those who have come to Christ individually, have to live twenty–four hours a day among their own people. And a new believer, in his struggle to assimilate his faith in Christ while trying to survive, as well as to confess his new–found faith in Christ as a Christ *bhakta* within his own community, faces lots of issues and problems. In order to help such a lay believer, we must step into his shoes and understand his problems. But most of the time, the full–time workers approach the issues as if they are their own problems. No doubt about it, the missionaries, in their ministry, face a lot of problems to relate the gospel properly. But they are definitely not living in the same situation that a new believer has to face. Most of the missionaries, particularly those who serve outside the tribal areas, live in cultural and social isolation from the people among whom they serve. Very few actually mingle with the people, trying to deeply identify themselves with them.

Since they need not and do not face most of the problems which a new believer is going to face, they should not hold themselves as the criteria but rather try to step into the shoes of their believers to face the challenges and problems with sympathetic understanding and real concern to help them to live as true *bhaktas* of Christ in their own situations. Several times, the missionaries failed by pulling the new believer out from his situation rather than encouraging and helping him to live as a *bhakta* of Christ in his own society. Full–time ministry is not the solution for the opposition and persecution that a new believer may face, though it almost seems to be the traditional evangelical solution. Are we more satisfied with one "convert" than with training him properly to reach a whole community through him?

Here, reaching a whole community through a "convert" should not be understood as trying to *win* others to Christianity, but rather to promote the righteousness of the Lord Jesus Christ in every community as Christ brings new values. Why I am saying this is that during a recent small meeting in Chennai, one convert himself, who is also a strong pro–church oriented man and a full time worker said, "A Brahmin convert should be allowed to remain in his family with his cultural and social identity only to *win* others for Christ." Such a strategy then will be rightly consider by the Hindu Fundamentalists as another trick played by the Christians to convert Hindus. But for me, allowing a person to remain in his family and community is neither a strategy nor a trick to convert others to Christianity but the rightful taking of new values into that community and society through that Christ *bhakta*.

Above all, why should a Christ *bhakta* be deprived his/her birthright to be a part of his own family and community? Introducing only Christ's values may be considered as liberal by the evangelicals since "conversion" to another community may be the only expression of authentic faith to them. But I don't find any biblical support for such a view. Likewise, some say that allowing a new believer to remain in his own cultural and social situation is part of "contextualization" of the gospel. Remember that contextualization is needed for an outsider to communicate the gospel in another culture. But if a Hindu is allowed to comprehend the gospel as a Hindu, then he need not "contextualize" the gospel but only naturally to live it out in his own cultural and social situation.

Respect for the Sentiments of the People
"Total man needs total gospel." This is true, but no one can understand the whole gospel in one sitting. "Share the complete message, including the second coming and judgment, because

this may be your last chance to preach or the last chance for your audience to hear." This is a simplistic concept, perhaps applicable to the so–called "revival" messages inside the church. But one cannot try to preach to his neighbor from Genesis to Revelation in one sitting. One must not even share immediately about a person's need for salvation using technical terms. First develop a good rapport, then create some curiosity and help a person to focus on his sense of need and lack of the fulfillment for which he is striving. This means that we need not immediately and directly point out that he is a sinner and teach other Christian doctrines. Rather avoid evangelical formulas, particularly those words which will hurt him and close his mind towards your efforts to approach him. Respect others' sentiments.

This goes not only in our approach to our neighbors but in our attitude towards new believers. Several Indian missionaries have respect neither for themselves nor for the new believers. They never trust the new believers nor allow them to develop. They always glorify the work done by the Western missionaries and criticize too much about the work that we are doing as Indians.

Attitudes to Missionaries

Simply exalting the Western missionaries and all they have done, irrespective of the negative side of their behavior, only shows our hypocrisy. See what kind of Christianity they have created in India – peculiar in the whole world. Whenever I touch the area of Western missionaries, immediately it is the Indian Christians who get annoyed. But I do not blame all the missionaries for all of the problems. Several of them were sincere and poured out their lives for God's sake in this country. I bow before their commitment and zeal, which I myself lack in several areas. But more than a few of them harmed the cause of Christ in this nation, and some of them wantonly and deliberately did so. Many lay people from poor backgrounds came as simple evangelicals to share the gospel (not just to preach) and always remained humble and helped the people to come forward both spiritually and socially, yet even these were not without their blind spots. But others came with the pride of empire and imposed Western ecclesiastical structures over which they presided in unbiblical hierarchies.

At present, some efforts are being made to present the truth of mission history without bias. But on such an emotional theme, it is very difficult for writers to overcome the influence of their own prejudices. For example, both Arun Shourie's recent book: *Missionaries in India: Continuities, Changes, Dilemmas* (ASA Publications, New Delhi, 1994) and Vishal Mangalwadi's response to him in his book: *Missionary Conspiracy: Letters to a Postmodern Hindu* (Nivedit Good Books, Mussoorie, 1996) are worth reading. But both of them became easy victims to their own prejudice while attempting to present the truth. (Readers will no doubt note the prejudices of this book more clearly than I myself can see them.) However much truth may hurt, a lie cheats, a half–truth destroys and not telling the whole truth disappoints.

Attitudes of Missionaries

It is often embarrassing to read what missionaries said about India and about Indian Christians. Sita Ram Goel, a bitter and often biased critic of church and mission (yet one from whom much might be learned) gives many examples:

> The mission had made no secret of the low esteem in which it held the natives of every description. A conference of foreign missionaries held at Calcutta in 1855 had proclaimed that the natives were known for "their deficiency in all those qualities which constitute manliness."[30]

> Another conference of foreign missionaries held at Allahabad in 1872 noted with concern that "Many or most of the 'educated native Christians' are showing feelings of 'bitterness, suspicion or dislike' towards the European missionaries" and "warned these radicals that as long as the native Church was economically dependent on European funds, it would be more proper for them to display patience with regard to independence."[31]

> Hindu converts, who had been ignored or insulted in an earlier period, are being raised from the dead and hailed as harbingers of Indigenization. Now we hear a lot about Krishna Mohan Banerjea, Parni Andy, Kali Charan Banerjea, J. G. Shome, A. S. Appaswami Pillai and Sadhu Sunder Singh....The mission has staged resurrection of those whom it had crucified earlier.[32]

Here is a similar case from a noted bishop:

> I recall how years ago a young missionary told me of what he called the
> impudence of an Indian clergyman, who was a graduate of one of the
> Indian universities, in going forward to shake hands with him. "This man,"
> he said, "thinks that because he is a graduate and has put on European
> costume, I must shake hands with him!"[33]

Of course though foreign missionaries have left (officially
only) India, still in some cases, they have their own way of doing things in Indian churches even today. Several churches and
missions are still under their direct control and they want to
see that Indians dance according to their tunes. This is not just
past history but a present reality, not only in India but in almost
all non–Western countries, particularly in Asia. The following
case study from Nepal, though from a slightly different context,
illustrates the foreign missionary domination over native Christians, which hinders the spontaneous expansion of the church.
I am thankful to Mark Johnson for his permission to share this
from private communication:

> This morning I was told a story. I thought it would be instructive to retell
> it to you. Some months ago, a wealthy architect and his wife were touring
> Nepal. At their hotel, they asked the waiter if he knew of any Christians.
> "Yes, there is one fellow who works here." Duly introduced, they asked
> about his church and pastor. "Why don't you come along this week?"
> they were asked. Meeting the pastor and seeing the church was an
> eye–opening experience for them. But they thought that there could be
> some improvements and so took the pastor out and explained to him that
> they could fund a new building. Not the sort of offer you have every day.
> One thing led to another. The couple saw a large plot of land and told the
> pastor to buy it. Last week, the congregation heard that they had been
> given a quarter of a million US dollars to build their new building. Consid-
> ering the average person in the congregation makes a monthly salary of
> $60 it was quite a sum. But what set me thinking more than the amount
> was something else. The pastor also received a box. In it was a pop–up
> cardboard model of the church building they were to build. "Church in a
> box" if you like, weird, but not so unusual as you might imagine. You see,
> models don't have to be made out of cardboard.
>
> Let me see if I can give an analogy. My son, Philip, was given a Meccano
> construction set for Christmas. In it are 450 pieces and an instruction
> manual to get you started. The instructions tell you how to use the tools
> and give some of the basic steps to building models. Then there are several
> models that are given with a step–by–step guide for building them. Philip

may follow the guide, but he may also use the pieces to build an original model of his own. Within the form that Meccano gives, he has freedom to express himself.

The disciples in Nepal have never had the freedom to express themselves. They have had "church in a box," whether quite literally as a cardboard model, or theologically as a set of predigested forms and formulations. These forms are like those models that are given in the Meccano guide. Only, instead of being presented as possibilities, they have been imposed as rules. This is the way it will be and no other.

The other day, I was talking to a visitor who was getting frustrated by what he sees as my idealism. Well, do we have to compromise our ideals? Is it all right to settle for semi—Biblical? The gospel is at stake. Most local and expatriate Christians cannot see what we are trying to get at. We have to live with that, and sometimes, like today, it is a struggle. But by God's grace, we will continue to hold up the hope that one day, a movement will emerge that will have the courage and wisdom to think outside the box and bring the message to their neighbors with full Biblical and cultural integrity.

Foreign Rule in Indian Churches

To quote a few examples: in Maharashtra, in the Free Methodist Church, they can elect two potential bishops for a single post, but in the end, the American Free Methodist Church, alone, has the "right" to appoint one of the two as bishop for the Indian Free Methodist Church.[34] Still today, the American Methodist Church sends "observers" for the elections of bishops in the Methodist Church in India. What business do these American Methodists have in the election of a bishop for the Indian Christians? If they are coming as observers to check that a free and fair election is conducted at the request of the Indian Methodist Church, then it is slavery; or if they are sent by the American Methodist Church, then it is imperialism.

I still cannot forget the mass surrender before the American director in the name of an altar call that I personally saw at a Free Will Baptist convention. I will not blame that American director because he gave a beautiful message. But the whole congregation was previously instructed about the "surrendering ceremony," and the person who gave the "altar call" just shouted in Hindi asking the people to commit themselves once again to

God. He never touched the points in the message. Only I and another disciple from a Hindu family (with whom I had already talked for two days, and influenced) did not join with the others in that surrendering ceremony. All the sheep bowed before this director and his wife, who was standing with a camera ready for that occasion and took several photos, no doubt for their promotional work back home, showing the number of people who accepted Christ through their ministry in India. Paul Kannan of Erode, while reading this manuscript, shared several such interesting stories, which confirm this kind of event, but cannot be related here due to constrictions of space. This is why I used to say that both Hindus and Muslims got their independence from British rule, but the Christians in India are yet to get it.

I am not against foreigners as such, but as a "free" Indian, I strongly oppose this dominating, imperialistic nature. They never allowed us Indians to worship, pray, think, share and form Indian churches. Now they are continuing it in a different form. In past days, the Western missionaries fought against those Indian *bhaktas* of Christ like Brahmabandab Upadhyay, Kali Charan Banerjea, R. C. Das and others in all their efforts to form Indian churches. By using their position and money, they practically crucified them. Sita Ram Goel gives a good example:

> It is true that English educated and high caste Hindu converts were prized by the mission, but if any Hindu convert acquired inflated notions about his intrinsic worth or his standing with the mission, he had to be put in his proper place. In 1856, Alexander Duff had denounced his own protégé, Lal Behari Dey, as the "ring leader of cabal" when the latter, along with two other Hindu converts, requested admission to the Committee of the Scottish Church Mission in Calcutta.[35]

When Sadhu Sunder Singh visited Europe, one bishop wrote and warned the European Christians against him. This prideful attitude from the imperialistic past is still affecting our churches in India. The attitude remains, but the color of the skin and nationality of the missionaries have changed. Sincerely following the Western directors, present native missionaries are equally unready to acknowledge the people among whom they serve as their equals.

Today's Missionaries Not Much Better

"Don't give much respect or treat the new converts as your equal. If you treat them as your equal, then one day they will usurp your position. Put them in their proper place." These were not the words of a foreign missionary but a "down–south" (the southern part of Tamil Nadu) missionary. Such missionaries do not want to see the new believers grow, so that they can take leadership in their field. They see a threat to their position and reputation in such growth. Each missionary wants to become a *jamindar* [lit. landlord] in his respective field. That is why too often the new converts feel suffocated as their freedom of expression and thinking are curbed in the name of protecting their faith by the churches. Dr. Rokhaya shared his experience on this line:

> I started to think: What if all Nepalis become Christians, as our church leaders would like to see? What would be left of our culture, of our colorful traditions, of our ethnic diversity? What about politics and literature? I realized that this would be a dangerous trend. At the same time, I became conscious of the fact that I actually was given very little freedom. The church provided guidelines in almost every field of life. At that time, I wouldn't even think of buying a news magazine or watch TV. Everything had to be Christian, from the pictures on the wall to the books on the shelves. I realized I was sitting in a prison, as I did when I was a Hindu, only this time with even less freedom.[36]

When I met Rokhaya in person, he even said, "At the time of the Holi festival, when all our neighbors are joyfully playing colors, our children sat inside the house and saw it with tears in their eyes. We could not send them out to play because it would be immediately reported in our church and severe action would be taken."

"We don't find deep commitment in their lives, so how can we trust them in these matters" is the common missionary statement. This is not my imagination, but the documented report of John S. Thannickal in his doctoral research on ashrams in reference to the Christa Panthi Ashram of the Mar Thoma Church in Sihora, M.P.:

> Christ's example of incarnation teaches us that foreignness in mission must
> be shed. The Ashram could well have reduced its foreignness had it re-
> cruited some Hindi—speaking Madhya Pradesh Christians into their team.
> It is appalling to note that in the 30 years of its existence, no north Indian
> Christian was included in their missionary team! The present list of Sihora
> Ashram members shows that all come from Kerala.

The author interviewed a research associate of the Mar
Thoma Mission concerning this serious deficiency in their missionary stewardship. The answer was typical of foreign missions
a quarter of a century ago. "There is no qualified Christian
among the converts to enter the Ashram," was the answer....The
Mar Thoma Church needs to realize that being Indian does
not mean being indigenous. A truly indigenous church should
be able to act like leaven in dough (Luke 13:21). In the process
of interaction the form of the leaven disappears and the dough
takes over the essence.[37]

Even if it is true that there is lack of commitment in new
believers' lives, who is to be blamed for this? Missionaries clearly
lack something, as they are not inspiring others to true discipleship. If we are in a position to say as Paul said, "Follow my example, as I follow the example of Christ" (1 Cor. 11:1) then we
can see the same commitment in our believers' lives. "The disciple is not above the *guru*" (Mt. 10:24, an obvious paraphrase).

Religion or Discipleship?

Present Christ and not Christianity, particularly not your denominational "churchianity." Christianity with all its nominal-
ism and "Western *masalas*" (priestly robes and hierarchical titles,
etc.) can hardly be considered better than the other religions.
And particularly if your neighbor is a Hindu, he has his own
dharma to follow (which is not "religion"). According to Hinduism one cannot follow another's *dharma* (Gita 3:35;[38] here also
dharma is not religion) because he has his own *dharma* to follow
as he is born in it. And according to him, *dharma* (rather than
being religion) is his life's dispensation based on his past *karmas*.
Show him how Christ would help him to overcome his *karmas*

and will lead to his particular fulfillment for which he is striving, based on his own personality.

Organized Religion or Society

In India, society is organized, and religion is not. The Hindus have neither a pope nor a bishop to guide them in their religious affairs. Taking care of their religious rituals is the duty of their priests, like that of the appointed pastor in churches. But Hindus never accept any "appointed" religious leader as their spiritual *guru*. All their *acharyas* (teachers) and *gurus* are recognized and accepted voluntarily and are not "appointed" by any authority. In the case of those selected leaders of any tradition (like that of the Sankaracharyas), one has complete freedom either to accept him or to reject. One of the most refreshing aspects of Hinduism is the freedom of choice it allows an individual (see Gita 18.63). (See also the section below on Hindu Freedom of Spiritual Choice.)

For a typical Hindu, the *pandit* (Hindu priest), *padri* (Christian pastor) and *maulvie* (Muslim clergy) are not spiritual *gurus* and *acharyas* but religious brokers taking care of people belonging to the respective religion, especially in their social obligations connected with religious ceremonies related to birth ("hatch"), marriage ("match") and death ("dispatch").

When the European missionaries came to India, they brought with them an organized religion and tried to impose it in an organized society and it never worked out. Hindus leaders like Raja Ram Mohan Roy and Keshab Chandra Sen, who, following the pattern of Western Church systems, tried to organize Hindu religion (called Renaissance Movements) ended in failure, e.g. Brahma Samaj, Prarthana Samaj, Church of the New Dispensation (Nava–vidhan), etc. The moment a few people decide to follow Christ, we immediately organize them into a religious structure with a particular denominational brand. But, as Dr. Robert Schmidt says, this "perversion of the Gospel happens whenever people, out of pride, wish to build organizations, traditions, and institutions in which they can find human security and status." [39]

But organized religion will never appeal to an average Hindu. If we want to see the kingdom of God among the Hindus, we must follow the pattern of spontaneity seen in the early church. Of course, as all gathering requires some kind of coordination, the appointing of elders and deacons in the early church is understandable and equivalent leadership roles will develop today. But "organizing" people under a denomination name is unbiblical. Yet the tragedy in India is that the Christian religion is organized according to denominations as in the West among whom there is severe competition to extend their own kingdoms among the Hindus. Robert Schmidt is referring to the West, but still his words have relevance in India also:

> As we look over the religious scene in our day, it is depressing. The free gift of salvation in Christ is used almost universally as a "come on." It has degenerated into a trashy advertising gimmick used to "hook" people into someone's organization where they can be duly manipulated and used. God's justification was intended to make people whole and free, but we have used it to make people cogs in an organizational machine, numbers to be counted and about which to boast.[40]

Denominations

If Hinduism is a "parliament of religions," then Christianity is the "parliament of denominations." The moment a new denomination is started in Europe, within 24 hours, its branch shop will be opened in India, particularly in Tamil Nadu and Kerala.

If we justify our denominations (more than 20,800) as "unity but not uniformity," then the Hindus justify their sects as *avibhaktam vibhaktesu*, "the unity in the division."[41] The competition among the denominations always confuses Hindu minds. As Dr. Radhakrishnan aptly said:

> We start by claiming that Christianity is the only true religion and then affirm that Protestantism is the only true sect of Christianity, Episcopalianism the only true Protestantism, the High church the only true Episcopal Protestant Christian religion, and our particular standpoint the only true representation of the High Church view.[42]

It seems that within every denomination, members always carry their denominational stigma everywhere. The Free Will Baptist Church, in their three day convention, taught all their members (mostly sheep stolen from other folds) that they should tell others that they are Free Will Baptist Christians

– the emphasis is on the denomination and not on "Christian." Unfortunately, I too was there, and I made it clear to some of the members that they had really lost their free will by accepting such a strong denominational stigma. Recently, while I was talking with a doctor who is from a mission hospital in the North East he said, "I cannot understand all that you say about Hinduism because of my background as a Baptist." I gently pointed out that it is not his Baptist background but his animistic background that is the reason for it. Dr. Schmidt has an insightful and humorous comment on this area also:

> The prophets of the 20th century are not noted for their denominational loyalties. Who cares that much whether Martin Luther King, Jr., was a Southern Baptist or that Alexander Solzhenitsyn is Russian Orthodox? In speaking of his own denominational affiliation, Toyohiko Kagawa [of Japan] is reported to have said, "My English is not good. Every time I say 'denomination', it comes out like 'damnation.'"[43]

Once I saw a small booklet (I cannot give a proper reference as I did not keep it, considering it useless and not anticipating ever writing something like this) in which the introduction said it was prepared "in order to propagate Lutheran Christian Doctrines to the Hindus." As if what the Hindus are urgently in need of is "Lutheran doctrines" and not the gospel. Luther even said not to start any denomination in his name, but denying him and his Christ, people created "Lutheranity." Bruce Olson met this particular type of Churchianity: "They [his parents] had been upset when I first told them about the reality of Christ in my life. My father was particularly apprehensive about this. If it couldn't be explained in Lutheran terms, it wasn't understandable – or acceptable."[44]

By saying all these things, I am not against everything related to denominations. Denominations have become an unavoidable reality for both good and evil in Christianity today. And as long as we are going to be in this phenomenal world, we cannot avoid various evils in whatever forms they may come. But denominations become a stumbling block when they prevent a *bhakta* of Christ from growing more deeply and personally in the Lord, based only on the word of God. When one must first

grow as this or that particular denominationalist and secondly
only (not at the cost of his "ist") as a believer in Christ, all lovers
of the gospel should rise in protest as is done by Schmidt in the
following words:

> Are we against all organization? Is not organization necessary to get a job
> done? What about the concept that people willingly "covenant" together so
> that duties can be divided and shared equally among interested people?
>
> No concept for organization is more Biblical than that of the covenant. But
> the Biblical notion of covenant is very instructive to our denominations. In
> Biblical times, people entered into covenants when they knew the terms
> (Exodus 19 and 20). They were renewed for those who were not present
> the first time (Deuteronomy 4 and 5)....
>
> However, in the present large organizations of churches and denomina-
> tions, there is no way people can digest all of the constitutional and
> regulatory provisions of the organization. As a result, the organization
> does not have the consent and good will of all the people for its actions.
> This means that new motivations (often trashy) have to be provided. New
> regulations are promulgated. If personnel do not conform, they are fired.
> Denominations and organizations of themselves are not bad. Rather, the
> problem is coercive control. We submit that it is better to lose the organi-
> zation than to use a non—covenanted, coercive control to make it work.[45]

Above all, because of their denominations, "Christians witnessed to their divisions rather than to their unity in Christ." [46]
Instead of working for the expansion of the kingdom of God,
they are striving for the expansion of their own respective denomination. The only hope for the church lies in her death to
this division, so that she can resurrect in a new transformation
as the body of Christ, rather than remaining as Churchianity:

> Only when congregations and denominations are willing to die can there
> be a resurrection and renewal of the church in our day. We have tried gim-
> micks, personal evangelism, and social action. We have tried intellectual-
> ism and anti—intellectualism. We have rearranged institutional furniture.
> We have created special groups for evangelism and social action. We have
> continually added and added but have not repented of what we are now.
> God calls us not to increase our activity but to cease from sin. Our divisions
> are as sinful as our wasted resources of money and manpower. Above all,
> has been the towering pride in the structures we have built to reach into
> the heavens. From this can only come death. But that death, we might
> welcome if it means the resurrected life of a chastened church.[47]

Creedianity

What is Christianity in the first generation, in the second generation becomes *churchianity*; in the third generation it is *creedianity* and in the fourth generation *Christo–paganism* or *Christian heathenism*. (Just read any American or European secular magazine and you can very well understand about the last two.) Of course *crossianity* is common in every generation – just wear a cross to show that you are a Christian ("take up the cross and follow," Mt. 16:24)

Some denominations seem to make their creed more important than personal faith in Christ. Creeds have a place as they give verbal form to the doctrines of respective denominations, and doctrines are essential as they give solid ground for one to express his beliefs. But when doctrines, replacing personal faith and experience (which seem to be anathema and taboo in many Christian circles) become cold dogmas, then it becomes another form of idolatry that has been called *dogmatolatry* by Raimundo Panikkar. "Dogmas are necessary so long as we are intelligent beings, but we should beware of the danger of 'dogmatolatry." [48] The main and really only purpose of theology is to help a person to verbalize and better understand his experiential knowledge of God. So it is a mistaken notion to turn Christianity into "creedianity." It is tragic that some with limited inner experience with Christ still propound a particular denominational creed and doctrine and so create a subtle idolatry rightly called dogmatolatry.

Neither Jesus Christ nor the apostles gave any kind of dogmatic formulas for us to confess. The Bible is not a book containing some statements of faith or dogmas. It is rather a work manual, giving practical solutions to the problems that we face in real life – that being mostly in the context of interpersonal relationships. The history of creedal development in Western Christianity shows various valid reasoning behind at least some of the creedal statements. But the importation of these things to India is now widely acknowledged as misguided. Selvanayagam echoes many others when he writes, "Admittedly, Christian thinkers and preachers have not presented the Christian teachings in a way that would draw the attention of Hindus. The early missionaries, in India, presented the gospel burdened with doctrines and liturgies of their own traditions in the West." [49]

Hindu Freedom of Spiritual Choice

Though truly, we are all human beings, whichever part of the world we may live in, yet there will never be any uniformity despite this basic unity as human beings. People's approaches to the various aspects of life—spiritual, cultural, social, etc.—differ from place to place. As their worldviews differ, so do their approaches to all of life. So, simply imposing any particular church dogma will not appeal to a Hindu. In spite of her variety of religious, cultural and social aspects, India's approach to finding the basis for the world, both the phenomenal and non–phenomenal, is unique.

In Hinduism, personal freedom is given to every individual in the area of spirituality (what we call "religion," which is not *dharma*) in his pursuit of reality. "Thus has this wisdom, more secret than secrecy itself, been imparted to you by Me. Fully pondering it, DO AS YOU LIKE" (Bhagavad Gita 18:63).[50] No one can impose his ideas on others in the area of spirituality, however good and relevant it may be for him. As many souls, so many views, is the basic tenet. In this respect, a *guru* is not one's spiritual "authority" or "religious boss," but a fellow pilgrim, guiding as well as traveling together based on his experience. In areas of spirituality, *"anubhava* holds the *pramaana"* (experience holds the evidence).[51] And therefore, religion is and cannot be organized in India.

Organized Christianity

Without proper understanding of these facts in following their Western predecessors, present day Indian Christians are involved in implementing their traditional approach of converting the people into "organized Christianity." Their efforts may win several proselytes for a time being, but if they want to really see the coming of God's kingdom among Indians, they have to radically change their approach.

The moment a few people follow Christ, they are immediately organized as a religious (and soon communal) group. The first thing that is stopping further church growth, particularly among the non–tribals, is the church building. By constructing the church building, spiritual growth becomes limited to within the boundaries of the structured religion. In a Hindu home, religious teachings are given by the parents and elders, and there is no equivalent to the responsibility carried among Christians by a Sunday School teacher, youth group leader or pastor. Spirituality is learned within the framework of their social and cultural set up not under the guidance of any organized, appointed religious leader.[52] Those who want to defend their organized churchianity, in the name of *koinonia,* should contemplate the following inspiring remarks of Christopher J. H. Wright:

> *Fellowship* is the usual translation of the Greek *Koinonia,* which is itself part of a rich complex of words. A study of the root *Koinon–* in the New Testament, reveals that a substantial number of the occurrences of words formed or compounded from it either signify, or are in contexts which relate to, actual social and economic relationship between Christians. They denote a practical, often costly, sharing, which is a far cry from that watery "togetherness" which commonly passes as "fellowship." (e.g. Acts 2:42,44; 4:34; Rom. 12:13; 1 Tim.6:18; Heb.13:16; Ro.15:26,27; 2 Cor. 8:4; 9:13; Gal. 2:9f; Phil. 1:27; 4:15ff)[53]

Hindu Organized Society

In Hindu society, the maintenance of social order in the areas of breach of ethical and moral injunctions is the responsibility of the society itself. If a Christian is expelled by his church, another group is ready to accept him because the organized religion cannot exercise its influence beyond its limitation of religion. Whereas in Hindu society, an ex–communicated person has either to repent or to leave that society as society is strongly organized. A Hindu is one who belongs to a particular community, not related to his personal faith in his religious systems. He is more a "social animal" aiming for personal spirituality rather than one concerned about a religious system. As we have already noted, Indian

Christians too belong to a particular community irrespective of
their religious system, which in theory claims no discrimination
among the believers based on caste, race and wealth. "Filial piety
and family ties" and not any "ideological commitment" decides a
Hindu home and community (of course there are always exceptions to this general rule), as noted by Raychaudhuri:

> We read of a young man from Orissa who had become a Brahmo howling
> in misery as his father dashed his bleeding head against a wall. The poet Mi-
> chael's [Madhusudan Dutt] mother pined away when he converted to Chris-
> tianity. One had to be exceptionally strong and committed to risk the pain of
> such confrontations. No wonder that the reforms had only very limited suc-
> cess. Filial piety and family ties were a more powerful influence on modern
> Indian sensibility than any ideological commitment to social change.[54]

This can be seen from the fact that, even today in the 21st
century (that too even among the Christians), rarely will a young-
er brother or sister marry while an elder sibling is yet unmarried.

From Jerusalem to Salem, Tamil Nadu

Without having this understanding, Indian Christians, like the
Western missionaries before them, insist on imposing organized
religion and so strangle church growth, as numerous case studies
can demonstrate. Why did church growth stop at Marandahalli
and surrounding areas? The past local problems and existing
Christians are not the main reasons. Only one or two Udayar
families came to Christ and even most of them also later left
the church. Why? People in and around Marandahalli saw only
a structurally "organized Christianity" giving a separate social
identity, including creating a separate burial ground. Instead of
arranging baptism at Marandahalli, they made Bethel, in Salem,
as the Mecca for the new believers (now such a pilgrimage has
stopped). To put it simply, "organized churchianity" stopped
church growth there. This is not only in Marandahalli. Around
Dharmapuri, as well as in down south, in the existing and old
fields, church growth is not as fast as it should be. Wherever a
church building is constructed, religion is organized; and there
the church growth is stopped. Make a heart–searching case
study of this by selecting a few other fields.

The main reason that church growth stopped is that such "organized churchianity" became culturally irrelevant to the people as non—essentials got priority over the gospel. Schmidt comments on this:

> Non—essentials include many things that we in the Western churches consider essential. The academic study of theology is really not essential, nor are public worship services, nor are musical instruments. Hymnbooks are not essential, nor are Sunday schools, nor are fellowship groups. Preachers are not necessary, nor are salaries, nor are church buildings, nor are budgets. In the final analysis, none of these are fundamental to the nature of the church. Yet, in spreading the Gospel, Western churches have brought all these things along with them. Many of these things are good; others are indifferent or bad. However, in sum, they have detracted from the message of the Gospel. What is worse is that they have come on so strongly that people in the third world have not had the opportunity to let their own culture supply them with more appropriate customs and structures. As a result, Western cultural baggage gives the churches a foreign flavor and tends to make them culturally irrelevant.[55]

The glorious gospel "which began in Palestine as a relationship with a Person, when it moved to Greece became a philosophy, then on to Rome and became an institution, spread all over Europe and became a culture and then moved to North America and became an enterprise." [56] And when it came to India, the gospel became European imperialism! Now in this 21st century, in the name of indigenization, what we have is personality cults within Christianity. And in all efforts to bring Hindus to such denominational Churchianity, there certainly will be little success.

Wherein lies the solution for this? Following the New Testament pattern we must allow a Hindu to remain as a Hindu culturally and socially, becoming a *bhakta* of Christ. Otherwise, conversion will remain a confusion as we force the new believer to live with impossible tensions in his society.

Evils in Hindu Society

Regarding "Hindu" social evils, like casteism and untouchablility, we cannot expect any miracles to take place overnight. It took nearly 1,800 years to abolish slavery from Europe. The racial problem still prevails in several Christian countries like

America, South Africa, Germany and England.[57] Casteism is
still in our own churches in south India, which we seemingly
cannot remove under the light of the word of God.[58] In this
area, instead of accepting our mistakes, we want to escape from
our responsibility to obey God by blaming outsiders. M. M.
Thomas quotes Manilal Parekh in this regard:

> Manilal Parekh finds fault with Western Protestant critics of caste churches
> who conveniently forget that even they have separate churches for the
> white and the colored people in America and Africa and to a large extent
> even in Asia itself:

> Deliberately and rejoicingly they compromise and make allowance with
> European culture, Western civilization and colonial imperialism, swallow-
> ing camel loads of these things, while they strain at a gnat of what they
> mistakenly think to be a compromise with the caste system or Hinduism
> in any form.[59]

Further Objections

"What you propose is nothing but yet another denomination,"
is the general criticism when this subject is raised. While others say, "We agree that there are several shortcomings in an
organized religion. But no denomination is going to be perfect.
So, in order to safeguard the faith of the believers, they must be
organized to some extent. Otherwise, lots of cults and sects, like
there are in Hinduism, will also come inside the churches."

To this, my answer is "Already we have more than 20,800
denominations and one more will not make much difference.
If you organize the new believers in the name of safeguarding
their faith, church growth will stop. The moment you construct
a church building and appoint a pastor and committee, then
all their time will be spent in fighting for authority inside the
church. True church growth stops, but biological growth (referred to as swelling by Subramania Iyer) continues and perhaps
some marriage Christians come in."

Regarding teaching, let the people recognize natural leaders,
and they will become the *gurus* for them. Find these people and
train them properly (that too locally in their social and cultural
context and definitely not in any seminary[60]), and allow them to

take care of the spiritual needs of the people. Note how different this is from organizing a denominational church and appointing a pastor just because he is a theological graduate. If there are 20 believers, divide them in four groups and let them study, pray and grow. If the number increases, further divide the group, but never gather them all under one roof especially just to exercise denominational authority over them. "Compulsory seminary certification deprives Christians in a given place of the right to select their leaders from their midst on the basis of Scriptural qualifications," says Dr. Schmidt, and continues, "Local churches should again have various church leaders as they had in apostolic times, some prophets, some evangelists, some pastors and teachers for the equipment of saints and for the work of the ministry. (Ephesians 4:11)" [61]

"If we agree with you then what alternative do you have for us to gather and worship in the name of the Lord? We may deny the mainline denominations, but as gathering is inevitable, so is some kind of coordination resulting in administration, which paves the way to start another denomination. Above all, what about the sacraments of holy communion and baptism, which cannot be exercised in isolation. As someone has well said, 'A Christian without a Church is like a bee without a hive.'" These are genuine questions, which need to be resolved. But most of the time, the answer that is given is based on their respective church (denominational) tradition and not necessarily from the Bible.

For example, "We should realize that any small group of Christians can celebrate the Lord's Supper as a *normal part of home life* or group living. Furthermore, they can select any of their fellow believers to serve as celebrant." [62] Though I am against the ecclesiastically organized and institutionally Christianized [Western] denominational churches, I am not against the concept of the body of Christ since, as Rev. G. S. Mohan wrote to me, "The Christian [i.e. biblical] faith is lived, enjoyed and fulfilled in the midst of people and with people and not in isolation." [63] Likewise, I am certainly not against "congregational worship," which is quite common among Hindus, also. But when denominations and buildings threaten real church growth, there must be serious thought towards some alternatives. As "watery fellowship" (cf. Wright above) does not equal real *Koinonia*, proper alternatives should be tried rather than blindly following church traditions. And above all, what is the hope for the "Churchless Christianity?"

Churchless Christianity

Herbert E. Hoefer, in his excellent book *Churchless Christianity* (William Carey Library, 2001) brings to the attention of the church and Christians that there are larger numbers of followers of Christ among the Hindus than there are in the churches in Tamil Nadu. And after thorough scientific research, he gives a call to the church to do something for these "Churchless Christians" in Hindu society; to seek after them and provide fellowship and encouragement to them. But our fear is that in the name of providing fellowship and encouragement, there will be the organizing of these Christ *bhaktas* in Hindu community under the Christian and even denominational labels. (On the other hand, even after 40 seminars presenting his information to Christian leaders, it seems that almost no one did anything practical to help these other sheep of Christ; which is perhaps preferable to giving them harmful "help," but still reflects very poorly on the spiritual state of the Christian church.)

By affirming the validity of the "Churchless Christian" phenomena Hoefer is not promoting the concept of "secret believers." Similarly, some get confused over our concept of "living as Hindu Christ *bhaktas*" in our respective communities. They say, "In order to avoid persecution as well as seeking worldly benefit and security, you do not obey God's call to leave the darkness and come to the light. (1 Pet. 2:9)" But the darkness and light here are spiritual, not communal; and the reason for us to keep our Hindu identity is to take the gospel inside our respective communities as leaven in the dough. This is possible when our own people realize that following Christ does not mean changing community allegiance. Unlike Western countries, here in India, particularly it is the community which holds the key both for our identity and survival and not personal religious faith and voluntary associations. It is not merely for survival, however, but because of our birthright, that we want to keep our Indian identity, which is always related with community identity.

Community and Communalism

At the same time, we must be aware of "the present policy of politicizing religion and communalizing politics." [64] To achieve some political gains, almost all the political parties in India are in one way or another involved in this process. The recent crisis in south Tamil Nadu between Devendra Kula Velalar (their leader is Mr. John Pandian) and Devar communities is the best example for this. Both the common people (even belonging to these communities) and their communal leaders agree that politicians want to see that communities remain divided on a communal basis, so that they can "warm their hands in a burning house." Yet for temporal gains and in the name of opposing the so–called brahminical oppression, some community leaders join hands with the politicians. Of course oppressive brahminism should be opposed, but not by making way for politicians to fish in troubled waters. (Some on the other hand, say that in order to lift their Dalit community, which they think is possible only through political power, they are ready to take help from any political party, however communal they may be.) A true Christ *bhakta* wants for the sake of gospel to keep his community identity, so that he can share with his own people; but he will oppose the negative side of communalism which threatens our national integrity.

Communalism is, of course, not only an Indian problem. Whenever I meet someone from England, if I ask, "Are you British?" they would prefer to say, "I am Scottish, Welsh, Irish, English," etc., rather than to claim a common British identity. The way in which such communalism was handled while maintaining national integrity in Britain is a lesson from which India can learn. [65] But these are wider national issues. That Christianity in India has been developed in opposition to existing communities, thus becoming itself thoroughly communalized, is one of

the great tragedies of mission history. (The failure of present day
Christians to recognize and grapple with the implications of this
communalization is perhaps an equally great tragedy.)

Christ's warning of the salt losing its savor is not our problem; rather that the salt sits in a lump and is not spread out
to do its flavoring or preserving work; the leaven is not in the
lump but is carefully removed and preserved (and thus rendered
useless). That is why Dalit leaders (even including the great
Dr. Ambedkar) refuse to become Christian; they cannot see
that caste prejudice has been removed even from the church,
let alone that the church could be leaven and free Indian society from this blight. Even today, though some Christian Dalits
are demanding a Dalit theology for their liberation, the Indian
Dalits are looking towards politicians for their liberation and
not towards the Christians or the church.

If Christians in India are able to demonstrate that they have
transcended their community identity, we too are ready to join
with them. But how this can ever be done is unimaginable. As
the integrity of the gospel is at stake, we want to keep our own
Hindu identity. Every Hindu Christ *bhakta* will testify with me
that we are doubly persecuted; the "Christian converts" who
have shifted their allegiance from one community to the other
face opposition from Hindus only, while we are understood by
no community. So we are not motivated by a desire to avoid
persecution, and neither is that the fact of our experience.

Congregation and Community

There is confusion among Christians about the church as a congregation and as a separate community, the former gathering in
worship and the latter existing within a society. The beauty of the
New Testament truth regarding this is that a follower of Christ
can recognize that he belongs to the body of Christ and therefore to the universal church while he can freely live as a member
of any sociological community. The Pauline concept of church
is emphatically not that of a separate community, as he clearly
wrote, "Nevertheless, each one should *retain* the place in life that
the Lord *assigned* to him and to which God has called him. This

is the rule I lay down in all the churches." (1 Cor. 7:17, emphasis added) The NIV Study Bible note says, "'Retain the place in life that the Lord assigned to him.' Each Christian is to live contentedly for the Lord in whatever economic, social and religious station in life God has placed him. See v. 18 for example." [66]

But this does not mean that we are justifying private faith by appealing to membership in the universal church. A congregational or body life expression of faith in Christ is essential for truly biblical discipleship. But if there is an area where Western Christianity is weak, it is in its ecclesial structures. Both the proliferation of denominations and the tying down of body life to Sunday morning meetings are (or should be) an embarrassment to anyone who is biblically literate. Should there not be much more radical openness to the possibility of whole new structures and patterns developing that might prove vastly more biblical than the anemic Western church models which are imposed as biblical and essential?

We too agree that Christ is the head of the church, and we are not loyal to him if not loyal to his church; but which church is this? Mere institutions? Those who belong to their respective denomination will love their institutions and the traditions and the history they represent. They may even quote the verse, "Christ loved the church and gave himself up for her" (Eph. 5: 25); but we know that what Paul means here is definitely not the institutions that developed in Western Christendom. Christians too easily read later Western "Christian" concepts of "church" into the New Testament references, which is clearly wrong and leads to serious distortions of biblical faith.

The Westernized Indian church denominations (like American Baptist, American Methodist, German Lutheran, Greek Orthodox, Syrian Jacobite, etc.) are called churches, yet they came as part of Western Christendom and hence are not really churches in a true biblical sense. As Kenneth Myers says (in his post–modern American context of course):

> Christendom was a cultural phenomenon, not simply a spiritual one. The death of Christendom is not the death of Christianity. Christendom was not the church; it was a generally friendly cultural setting for the church.

What we are seeing now is only the death of a culture with a mixture of Christian and pagan assumptions. In fact, one could argue that the death of Christendom (or the death of a supposed "Christian America") is an opportunity to preach Christ clearly without the confusion of cultural assumptions. However, that means that the church has lost a long–time friend whose tutelage was repaid with defense and an honored seat at the head of the cultural table. It is sad, but not fatal.[67]

Faith and Community

No faith, Hindu or Christian or biblical, can be exercised in isolation. The too common comparison of the Christian church as a community with Hinduism as a highly individualistic religion is an entirely false antithesis. Hinduism is far from void of community expressions of faith and life. For example, in Vedic times, a householder could not perform *yajna* (sacrifice) without the cooperation of his wife if he wished to attain heaven.[68] Generally, both the husband and wife and even children are considered to share in the virtues and vices of each other.[69] Likewise, a king shared one sixth of the merits of his people for protecting them and aiding them to follow their respective *dharmas*, and in case of their sin (*adharma*), if he did not punish them, the demerit was also his. That is why, in a Hindu kingdom, the king was considered as a deity. Except in the case of a *sanyasi* (one who renounced), the whole life of Hindu society is a corporate affair striving for *dharma, artha* (wealth), *kama* (pleasure) and *moksha* (liberation). Especially the *samskaras* (ceremonies) are always family and community celebrations, with both their religious and social significance; this is directly coming down from the ancient Vedic tradition of the necessity of the wife for *yajna* mentioned above. Even in the case of *sanyasis,* there existed and still exist both Brahmanical monastic communities (*dasanaamis* of Sankara *mathas* and Sri–Vaisnava *mathas*) and non–Brahmanical monastic communities.

Comparing Hindu (largely individualistic) *puja* [worship] both in the temple and home with Christian worship under a roof in the name of "church" reveals a poor understanding of both. In this area also, the Hindus have corporate worship in their temples; *bhajans, kirtans, satsanghs* etc. etc., of course with their own ideologies. As Selvanayagam writes, "It is not true that Hinduism is always an individualistic religion. The communion of saints, for example, is theologically significant as is evident in the Saiva devotional texts." [70] He further illustrates the point by saying, "For Christians, it is fascinating to note that only a reconciled community can worship in the village [Hindu] shrines. No celebration of a festival can take place as long as there is a breach in the community. Common cooking and sharing is one of the most vivid expressions of community bond." [71]

Biblical Patterns and Principles

All the points above demonstrate again the need to deeply understand both biblical and present day social contexts in order to faithfully represent Christ and His gospel. Thankfully, the Bible never gives a pattern to blindly imitate but rather gives principles to adopt in varying situations. This does not mean situation ethics and the bending and twisting of absolute principles and commands, which are of course also present in the Bible. But in the particular area of ministerial methods and issues related to culture and society, the Bible gives no rigid pattern to follow. Constant rethinking and revision, constant learning from the Bible, history and particular cultural and religious contexts are essential. If this chapter (and book) stimulates such rethinking and revision it will have served its purpose.

Notes

1 Hesselgrave, David J., *Today's Choices for Tomorrow's Mission: An Evangelical Perspective on Trends and Issues in Mission*, Academie Books, Zondervan Publishing House, Michigan, 1988, pg. 152.

2 Another convert who understood this problem facetiously asked me how one becomes a strong Christian; his answer was "by eating beef and talking against Hinduism."

3 Whaling, Frank, *An Approach to Dialogue with Hinduism*, Lucknow Publishing House, Lucknow, 1966, pg. 7.

4 Hesselgrave, D. op. cit., pg. 151. Cf. Selvanayagam's observations:

...it should be acknowledged that the missionary contribution to the study of Hinduism is praiseworthy....But unfortunately, this contribution seems to have two upsets. On the one hand, Hindus have not shown similar interest in the sympathetic study of Christianity. On the other hand, Christians with missionary zeal feel it is unnecessary or even dangerous to study Hinduism with empathy. The missionary heritage of studying Hinduism and other religions is followed by the theological institutions of India. But its effect on the missionary approach of the Church, on its biblical studies and theologizing is minimal. (Selvanayagam, op. cit., pg. 128)

5 Bruce Olson, *Bruchko*, Creation House, Lake Mary, FL, 1995, pp. 133–34.

6 Cf. G. U. Pope: "...Nothing....can be expected to live and be effective among a people if not expressed in their own vernacular language, the 'vulgar tongue', in which they were born." (*The Tiruvacagam*, Oxford University Press, 1900, pg. xii.)

7 Davis, J. Merle, "Missionary Strategy and the Local Church," *International Review of Missions* 38, 1949, pg. 408; quoted from Thomas, M. M., *The Acknowledged Christ of the Indian Renaissance*, SCM Press Ltd., London, 1969, pg. 304. Cf. also Bruce Olson's experience:

I was eager for Bobby to tell them. He could do it more effectively than I, I was sure. I tried to encourage him to share his experiences, and was upset when he didn't. Was it because he didn't care enough about the other Motilones? I couldn't be sure.

But I was trying to squeeze him into "the mold" and didn't realize it. News has no real significance to the Motilones until it's given in a formal ceremony. In my excitement over Bobby's spiritual experience, I wanted him to do things the way they would have been done in North America. I wanted to call a meeting and tell about Jesus, or corner his friends and explain what Jesus now meant to him. But thank God he waited until he could do it the Motilone way.

...The home was deathly still, except for Bobby's wailing song and Adjibacbayra's repetition. People were straining their ears to hear. Inside me, however, a spiritual battle was raging. I found myself hating the song. It seemed so heathen. The music, chanted in a strange minor key, sounded like witch music. It seemed to degrade the Gospel. Yet when I looked at the people around me, and up at the chief swinging in his hammock, I could see that they were listening as though their lives depended on it. Bobby was giving them spiritual truth through the song. Still I wanted to do it my way...until I heard Bobby sing about Jesus giving him a new language. "Can't you see the reality that he is giving to them?" "But Lord," I replied, "why am I so repulsed by it?" Then I saw that it was because I was sinful. I could love the Motilone way of life, but when it came to spiritual matters I thought I had the only way. But my way wasn't necessarily God's way. God was saying, "I too love the Motilone way of life. I made it. And I'm going to tell them about my Son in my way." I relaxed, able at last to find real joy in Bobby's song. It continued for eight hours, ten hours. Attention didn't slacken.... Finally, after fourteen hours, they quit singing and climbed wearily down from their hammock. (Olson, B., op. cit. pp. 151–53)

8   Olson, op. cit. pg. 169.

9   Griffiths, Michael, *Give Up Your Small Ambitions*, pp. 103, 112.

10 For a detailed study of de Noblili see A. Sauliere and S. Rajamanickam, *His Star in the East*, Gujarat Sahitya Prakash, Gujarat, 1995, and also for a different and critical perspective *Disputed Mission* by Ines G. Zupanov, Oxford University Press, New Delhi, 1999.

11 Staffner, Hans, *Jesus Christ and The Hindu Community*, Gujarat Sahitya Prakash, Anand, 1987, pg. 237. Cf. also David Ludden: "Major General Stockley Warren, who retired in 1885, reminisced in these terms on his reaction to a Muslim 'coolie' who would not have brandy for medicinal purposes: 'These men I presume we shall ultimately civilize, make them Christians and Drunkards, and lead them to liberty'." (*Making India Hindu: Religion, Community, and the Politics of Democracy in India*, ed. David Ludden, Oxford University Press, New Delhi, 1996, pg. 187)

12 "The name Paranghi given to the Portuguese does not mean Christian. The Saint Thomas Christians are not called Paranghis but Nazaranis, and the new converts are called Maargakaarer or men of the law, the Armenian Christians are known by the same name. Paranghi means, both here and in Madurai, a barbarous and beastly individual without any education... .Therefore any Portuguese can deny in all truth that he is a Paranghi, *a fortiori* we, who are not Portuguese, can deny it on oath. The reason why that name creates such difficulties, among certain Fathers is that they do not know what it really means." (letter of Archbishop Ros to Aquaviva of the Society of Jesus from Cochin on November 28, 1612; Sauliere, op. cit. pg. 213)

13 Ibid. pg. 43.

14 Ibid. pg. 44.

15 Thomas, M. M., op. cit., pp. 258–59.

16 Hoefer, Herbert E., *Churchless Christianity*, Asian Programme of Advancement of Training and Studies (APATA), India, and The Department of Research & Publications, Gurukul Lutheran Theological College and Research Institute, Madras, 1991, pg. 98. Harijan is the Gandhian term for "untouchables", today mostly called Dalits.

17 Ibid. pg. 55.

18 See for example the article "Caste and Church," by Dr. Ebenezer Sundarraj, in *India Church Growth Quarterly*, vol. 7 no. 2, April–June 1985: "In India, the roots of castes are racial, occupational and economic, migrational and religious." (pg. 81) Giving "few humble recommendations from mission field experience" he suggests, "Church's preaching/pulpit calendar must allot one Sunday a year as 'Brotherhood Sunday' for preaching against Brahminic Caste System in the Church" and "Appointment of religious staff like pastors, bishop, missionary, etc. and all ecclesiastical leaders like committee members of diocese, synod, federation, etc. must be made conditional on taking a spouse of 'lower' caste on marriage to his child or grand child, whoever is unmarried, after 10 years of his appointment." (pg. 83) Though he said all this with right motive, the fact is that

the church remains the same. And still worse, in Chennai, several Nadar based churches separated from the Church of South India because of this caste problem (supposed Dalit domination) and joined with the Anglican Church. For an analysis of Christians in relation to Indian communities see H. L. Richard, "Rethinking Community," *Dharma Deepika*, July 2000, pp 51–58.

19   Griffiths, Michael, op. cit., pg. 137. And G.U. Pope says, "For many years I have not ceased to say – there in India, and here in Oxford – to successive classes of students, 'You must learn not only to *think* in Tamil, but also to *feel* in Tamil, if you are to be intelligible and useful among the Tamil people.'" (op. cit., pg. xi, italics original)

20   When Motilone tribal land was gradually encroached on by outsiders, the people faced the issue of whether to retreat or fight for their right to keep their land. They went to Bruce Olson, who instead of giving any teaching, instruction or advice to the Motilone tribes, said that whatever decision they would take, he would stand with them. In that given situation, "resist not evil" or "turn your cheek" would not help, so instead of imposing any of his ideas in the name of biblical teaching, Bruce Olson allowed the people to take their own decision. (Bruce Olson, *Bruchko*, op. cit. pg. 184.)

21   Dunning, quoted by Oswald Sanders in *Spiritual Leadership*, pg. 51.

22   S. Sudarsan Thomas (FMPB), letter to Dayanand Bharati, Dadri, Haryana, 19th December 1992. About the nature and need of such seminary training Robert Schmidt says:

Church control exercised through obligatory seminary education of church leaders is contrary to Biblical example (Acts 14:23) and substitutes academic qualifications for those of personal morality, and aptitude in teaching and combating error (I Timothy 3:2–7; Titus 1:7–9).

If one analyzes the qualifications of church leaders in 1Timothy 3:3–13 and Titus 1:7–9, one is amazed to find so few intellectual qualifications. There are eleven moral qualifications, one moral—intellectual, one of experience, and two concerned with reputation. In the second list recorded in Titus 1:6–9, there is but one moral intellectual qualification, namely, "holding to the faithful word." Regardless of any denomination's teachings on the subject of the public ministry, nearly all require long training at universities, seminaries, or church colleges. (*The Transformation of the Church,* Transformation Media, Oregon, 1999, pg. 28.)

23   Cf. Bhagavad Gita 13:25: "Other dull witted persons, however, not knowing thus, worship even as they have heard from others; and even those who are thus devoted to hearing, are able to cross the ocean of mundane existence in the shape of death."
(Janadayal Goyandka (tr.), Gita Press, Gorakhpur, pg. 570).

24   Cf. J.N.D. Kelly: "Most significant of all, however, is the fact that the Church of the fathers was set in the complex cultural environment of the Roman Empire. This means that, although drawing on its own unique sources of revelation, Christian theology did not take shape in a vacuum. The atmosphere in which it had to grow and develop was crowded with religious, philosophical and even theosophical notions. To some of these it reacted violently, by others it was consciously or unconsciously affected. Some degree of familiarity with this environment is indispensable to anyone

who hopes to appreciate the evolution of patristic thought." (*Early Christian Doctrines*, Second Edition 1960, Harper & Row, New York, pp. 5–6)

25   Quoted by Whaling, Frank, op. cit. pg. 20, from *Eastern Religions and Western Thought*, p. 305.

26   S. Radhakrishnan, *The Principal Upanishads*, Oxford University Press, Delhi, 1992, pg. 9.

27   In an article on Christian Vedantism, R. Gordon Milburn wrote: "Christianity in India needs the Vedanta. We missionaries have not realized this with half the clearness that we should. We cannot move freely and joyfully in our own religion because we have not sufficient terms and modes of expression wherewith to express the more immanental aspects of Christianity. A very useful step would be the recognition of certain books or passages in the literature of the Vedanta as constituting what might be called an Ethnic Old Testament. The permission of ecclesiastical authorities could then be asked for reading passages found in such a canon of Ethnic Old Testament at divine service along with passages from the New Testament as alternative to the Old Testament lessons." (From *Indian Interpreter*, 1913, quoted by S. Radhakrishnan, *The Principal Upanishads*, ibid. pg. 19.)

28   Clooney, Francis X., *Theology after Vedanta: An Experiment in Comparative Theology*, State University of New York Press, Albany, pg. 38.

29   de Smet, Richard V., "The Gita in Time and Beyond Time," from *The Bhagavad Gita and the Bible*, Unity Books, New Delhi, 1972, pg. 10.

30   Goel, Sita Ram, *Catholic Ashrams: Adopting and Adapting Hindu Dharma*, Voice of Truth, New Delhi, 1988, pg. xxv.

31   Ibid. pp. xxv–xxvi, quoting from Kaj Baago, *Pioneers of Indigenous Christianity*, CLS, Madras, 1969, pg. 3.

32   Ibid. pg. xxxix.

33   V. S. Azariah at Edinburgh 1910, quoted by R. E. Hedlund in *Roots of the Great Debate in Mission*, ELS, Madras, 1981, pg. 177.

34   A Free Methodist pastor confirmed to me the truth of this after I had heard it from others while ministering in Yavatmal.

35   Goel, Sita Ram, op. cit., pg. xxv.

36   Rokaya, op. cit.

37   Thannickal, John Samuel, *Ashram: A Communicating Community*, a dissertation presented to the faculty of The School of World Mission and Institute of Church Growth, Fuller Theological Seminary, May 1975, pp. 272–73.

38   "One's own duty, though devoid of merit, is preferable to the duty of another well performed. Even death in the performance of one's own duty brings blessedness; another's duty is fraught with fear." Gita 3:35, Goyandka, op. cit. pg. 169.

39   Schmidt, op. cit. pg. 5.

40   Ibid. pg. 22. Further, Schmidt comments: "…Most mission endeavors are the extension of the church as an institution. Too often evangelism is not

really thought to be successful unless it has added members to a church or group or claim that so many people turned out for this function or that" (pg. 25).

41   Tilak, B. G., *Srimad Bhagavadgita–Rahasya*, Tilak Brothers, Poona, 7th Edition, 1986, pg. 591.

42   Quoted by Whaling, Frank, op. cit. pg. 14.

43   Op. cit. pg. 64.

44   Olson, op. cit. pg. 30. About this Schmidt, a Lutheran theologian, says, "…instead of giving their members the freedom to make their own decisions, church bodies like the Lutheran Church – Missouri Synod are insisting upon more denominational control." (op. cit. pg. 1)

45   Op. cit. pp. 26–27.

46   Schmidt, ibid. pg. 1.

47   Ibid. pg. 55.

48   Panikkar, Raimundo, *The Unknown Christ of Hinduism*, Darton, Longman & Todd, London, 1981, pg. 54.

49   Selvanayagam, I., op. cit. pg. 136. Cf. Schmidt also: "Most confessions and creeds were written for a specific situation in history. Like many of us, however, they have the tendency to put on extra weight over the years. Even after the situation they addressed has long gone, the creeds live on. They also begin to pick up functions that their authors never intended them to have. Most of the time, they were put forward as positive theses, identifying a certain position. Later on, they became a test of orthodoxy to which people must adhere or suffer expulsion." (op. cit. pg. 46) But Schmidt is not completely opposing all forms of creed. He even recommends a "provisional" creed to "accomplish a provisional goal. In this case it would be church fellowship among people at the local level. These confessions would be happy documents, freely created, and after their purpose had been accomplished, they could be happily destroyed….Such people would not need to speak about all aspects of the faith (indeed, what creeds do?), but only those which directly affected their fellowship together." (pg. 51)

50   Goyandka, op. cit. pg. 785.

51   This slogan "experience holds the evidence" is a complicated subject. According to the theological tradition of India regarding *pramaana* (evidence), it is not *anubhva* (experience) but rather scripture, which holds the final authority. But as we have seen above, when it comes to individual freedom, this slogan still gets prominence. So I use "experience holds the evidence" in regard to the freedom of an individual and not related to theological principle. Note also that this concept of "experience holds the evidence" received new emphasis and interpretation by Vivekananda, who on this theme created a lot of confusion, which continues to the present. On this subject see Rambachan, op. cit., *The Limits of Scripture*.

52   About this Schmidt says:

By replacing parents as the chief source of Christian education, the church, in effect, discourages Christian education in the home and communication between parents and their children on subjects of ultimate meaning and morality.

Several tragedies have come about because of the institutionalization of Christian education. The first is that there has come into existence a large gap between Christian knowledge and Christian living....Unless Christian education gets released from its bondage to the church and gets back into the home, it will be increasingly difficult for the teachers because it is largely irrelevant to the students.

The second tragedy is that question of ultimate meaning and morality are taken out of the family circle. When the big questions come up on death, suffering, and choice of vocation, few in the family are willing to approach them religiously. Religious subjects, except in the case of a few dedicated families are almost universally avoided....Harry Wendt, the notable Christian educator, has said that the difference between Jesus' educational methods and our own is this: While we educate children and play with adults, Jesus played with children and educated adults. (op. cit. pg. 57)

53 Christopher J. H. Wright, *Living as the People of God: The Relevance of O.T. Ethics*, IVP, London, 1983, pg. 98.

54 Raychaudhuri, Tapan, *Perceptions, Emotions, Sensibilities: Essays on India's Colonial and Post–Colonial Experiences*, Oxford University Press, New Delhi, 1999 pp. 12–13.

55 Op. cit. pp. 53–54. Cf. also Lipner's analysis of Keshab Chandra Sen position: "Christianity, at least the Christianity offered to India, was a different matter, in its doctrines and dress a western import, tending to 'denationalize' the Indian who adopted it." (Lipner, Julius J., *Brahmaband-hab Upadhyay: The Life and Thought of a Revolutionary*, Oxford University Press, Delhi, 1999, p. 59)

56 Rev. Dr. Samuel Kamalesan in the concluding message of his song cassette, "This is My Story," produced by Friends Missionary Prayer Band, Madras.

57 Note this tragic account of Caribbean Christian immigrants to England: "In the Caribbean, they were used to worship in a Church where the clergy and leadership were English and white, and so anticipated nothing but acceptance and even welcome in churches in Britain with whose liturgy and worship they were thoroughly familiar. They were disappointed. The racism they encountered in society, which denied them adequate housing, jobs for which they were qualified, and reasonable services and credit facilities (see the Political and Economic Planning Report on Racial Discrimination, 1967) was also present in the Church. Clergy from the Caribbean, returning to England on furlough or for retirement, were dismayed to find erstwhile faithful members of their flocks not in Anglican congregations but either reading their Bibles at home or members of immigrants' house–churches which eventually became the predominantly black independent churches which have taken root and now play an important part in the life of our society." (Wilfred Creydon, Chairman, Committee on Black Anglican Concerns, in Foreword, *Seed of Hope*, op. cit. pp. v–vi.)

58 The standard verse quoted in this area is Gal. 3:28, but does this verse really mean that in Christ we will loose our respective racial, social and cultural identity? What I think Paul refers to here is our theological position in Christ. But in the reality of life he never expected that Jews and Greeks

or free and slave would loose their social/racial identity. Such an aim is an empty ideal. Accepting the reality of the world, Paul still allowed them to keep their separate identity. Otherwise how can the words "no male or female" in this verse be interpreted?

59   Thomas, M. M., op. cit., pg. 258, quoting from Parekh, Manilal C., *Christian Proselytism in India: A Great and Growing Menace*, Rajkot, 1943, pp. 60f, 66. Cf. also Selvanayagam's comments on Ambedkar:

> More remarkably, Dr. Ambedkar openly denounced Hinduism for its oppressive caste structure and left it with nearly 3.5 million "untouchables" in 1956. But Christianity did not appear to be an option, not only because it was a foreign religion and caste was operative in the Churches, but also because the Christian converts from this section were unwilling to identify with their brothers and sisters outside in the society. The social content of conversion seems to continue in future. This should be challenging for both Christians and Hindus. (op. cit. pg. 120)

60   Cf. Schmidt: "Full–time seminary training can be useful for training teachers, scholars, and traveling missionaries, as long as non–seminary trained people are also eligible for church leadership positions, as they were in the New Testament. (Acts 14:23)" (op. cit. pg. 6)

61   Ibid. pg. 6.

62   Schmidt, op. cit. pg. 104, italics added. Further on this he says, "In nearly every denomination, people think it is necessary to have such an 'ordained' creature around for a legitimate celebration of the Lord's Supper. This denies the right of the universal priesthood of all believers to choose any fellow believer to administer the sacrament. It also has the effect of tying the church to expensive complex institutions such as seminaries, church buildings, and denominations. These institutions, in turn, have imprisoned the church's message for far too many years." (pg. 104)

63   Personal letter of Rev. G. S. Mohan, 1991.

64   Selvanayagam, op. cit. pg. 61.

65   See Richard Fox's analysis: "Local elites could use Welsh consciousness to support their demands for local economic and cultural development against the state, but the lobbying was on a national level and the terms of the competition were set by the national state. In the event, they won concessions – Welsh–medium schools, Welsh–language television, major capital inputs, and the like – but gave up political and sectarian community. I can end the Welsh case here, at the point where the bureaucratic state has co–opted Welsh identity and paid it off on its own terms." (Richard G. Fox, "Communalism and Modernity" in Ludden, op. cit. pg. 247.)

66   W. Harold Mare, "1 Corinthians," *NIV Study Bible*, Kenneth Barker, general editor, Zondervan Corporation, Grand Rapids, pg. 1742.

67   Myers, Kenneth A., "A Better Way: Proclamation Instead of Protest," in Michael Scott Horton, ed., *Power Religion: The Selling Out Of The Evangelical Church?* Moody Press, Chicago, 1992, pp. 54–55.

68   Cf. P. V. Kane on this point: "It is on account of the necessity of associating the wife in all religious acts that the hero Rama was compelled to celebrate sacrifices with a golden image of Sita by his side. Panini [IV.1.33] derives the word *patni* [wife] and says that it can be only applied to a wife

who shares in the sacrifice [and its reward]. It follows that wives who are not or cannot join with their husbands in *yajnas* are only *jayas* or *bharyas* [but not *patnis*]….It is on account of this close association of the wife in all sacrifices that the wife if she dies before her husband is burnt with the sacred fire or fires and with the sacrificial vessels and implements [Manu V.167–68, Yaj.I.89]….Vaisvarupa on Yaj. remarks that though the eldest wife alone is entitled to take part in religious rites, all wives [except a Sudra wife] may be cremated with the *srauta* fire." (op. cit. pp. 558– 559)

69   Wendy O'Flaherty points out that "The concept of the transfer of good and evil occurs throughout Indian texts on various levels of religious experience." (*Karma and Rebirth in Classical Indian Traditions*, Motilal Banarsidass, Delhi, 1983, pg. 67) Further, "The most significant transfers take place within the family, between husbands and wives, siblings, and parents and children….The wife's chastity is an integral part of her husband's *karma*; the chaste wife can release her husband from his sin (*Matsya Purana* 52.23–25). Like all *karma* transactions, this has a negative side as well: to destroy a man, destroy his wife's chastity." (pg. 29)

70   Op. cit., pg. 116.

71   Ibid. pg. 117.

CHAPTER THREE

SPECIFIC AREAS OF FAILURE

The gospel is never communicated until the message is understood.

The realization of this important fact has not yet fully dawned on us. Most Christians, irrespective of their denomination or organization, are always trying to pull the people up to their own level of understanding, rather than understanding the people first and adjusting to their level. Apart from the message as a whole, even the words and jargon they use hardly communicate anything to the people. Yet, most seem to take it for granted that, irrespective of the words and terms they use, the gospel message, on the whole, gets communicated.

When I shared this with a group of missionaries, most of them could not understand what I meant, nor could they appreciate the difficulty a Hindu would face in understanding the message we try to communicate. In order to help them realize the difficulty, I read aloud some of the notes I had prepared on the Bhagavad Gita and Upanishads. After reading only one page, most of them accepted that, though they could read it themselves and understand the language as a whole, they could not understand the subject in depth because most of the concepts and terms were new to them. I then asked them to step into the shoes of those to whom we do the same thing.

"Give the living water in an Indian bowl" has been a long time cry borrowed from Sadhu Sundar Singh. Though it has been raised time and again, very little seems to change. But surely the time has now come to seriously think and act in this direction. We have failed to communicate in our general presentation, in our worship, in our language and terminology, in our theology, and in relation to Hindu scriptures and the Indian nation. Each of these areas of failure will be examined, granting that there is much overlap between them. Suggested ways in which truly incarnational communication can be developed will be spelled out as well.

A. In Our General Presenation

During 1991, on Jesus *Jayanti* (Christmas) Day, I was with my parents. Along with my auntie, both my father and mother were watching the television programs in Tamil. Being Christmas Day, there were several programs with lots of carols and even a Christmas message. After nearly an hour of programs, I asked them, "Do you understand anything?" All in one voice, they said, "Not a bit." Then my mother, commenting on the programs, said something in Tamil, which cannot be translated into any other language: *oru ezhavum puriyala;* which might be put into English as "Not a hell do I understand." Then after saying this, she started opening and shutting her mouth imitating the singers in the choir (with their English songs and Tamil songs with Western music). Then she continued, "Today being Jesus *Jayanti* (I learned this phrase only from my mother!), why don't they sing some *bhajans* and worship Him? Furthermore, why do they open and shut their mouths in that way?" Now it should be acknowledged that some change has come in presenting Christmas programs in an Indian way, which is definitely encouraging. This year, the program was done using more typical Indian lyrics and Bharat Natyam (classical Indian dance) was even performed. It is very encouraging to see these art forms being used, and such indigenous presentations ought to be encouraged by the church.

We may worship the Lord in spirit and in truth, but if it is in Western ways, others in India will not understand it. Not only those Christmas songs, but even the person (bishop?) who shared the Christmas message used a lot of "pulpit Tamil" which only a Christian can understand. When Christians produce such programs in the mass media, they seem least bothered about communicating the message to people of other faiths. (The recent television serial "Bible Story," which by the grace of God was stopped, again illustrates the miscommunication. Those Hindus who might have seen this must have been wondering whether it was a Christian or Muslim program because so much Urdu language [more than 75%] was used, which the average Hindu can hardly understand.)

Worst of all, some among us insist on inviting foreigners to share the Christmas message in India. During 1990, when Billy Graham was sharing the Christmas message on television, I and I am sure many others, were deeply distressed. Why would Billy Graham preach on Christmas day on Indian television with his coat, suit, tie, and above all, with shoes on his feet and sitting on a sofa cross legged? What kind of impression would our people have gotten on seeing such a program?

I am not objecting to Billy Graham wearing Western dress or to his preaching (in English), but can we not find one Indian, who can sit on a stage in Indian dress and preach the same message, even in English? We cannot blame Billy Graham for this. If we approached him by saying, "We got permission from the government of India to broadcast a Christmas program on television, but it is a costly one. We want you to sponsor it, but we want to do it in an Indian way, so that the majority of the Indians of the other faiths who may see it can benefit," he no doubt would have approved of it and done as requested. However, I suppose we wanted to please Billy Graham rather than to reach our people, and of course it would not be right to use him.

The daily radio programs, for which crores [ten millions] and crores of rupees are being spent, are not much better. In Bangalore, while I was talking with a full–time worker serving in an organization with an emphasis on radio ministry about the need to communicate the gospel, he said, "No, brother, it is not like you think. Nowadays we receive lots of response from our listeners. This proves that we are communicating the gospel." When I asked him what "lots" means, he replied that they receive letters in the thousands. But he forgot that our country has reached 100 crore in population. Whereas they are satisfied in receiving responses in the thousands, and they are mostly from Christians! (This does not mean that I am against all the radio programs.)

Already, we saw the way Swami Vivekananda used biblical terms to communicate his Vedantic message to his American disciples. He may be wrong according to our emphasis on context in interpreting the Bible, but he was right in his approach in communicating his message to his audience. Even Muslims understand the value of contextualization and started not only to translate the Koran in local languages, but even to broadcast it in Indian languages. Today at the West Chintamani mosque in Trichy, one can hear daily, early morning preaching in simple Tamil from the Koran.

In the secular world, business people go to great efforts in communication to sell their products and gain permanent customers. On January 27th, 1992, I went to the shop called "Families" near Madavakkam in Kilpauk at Chennai. I had previously visited the shop several times. The owner is from the Coimbatore area and is a non–Brahmin. But when I wanted to buy one *papadam,* he did not recommend it, and in explaining its lack of quality, he talked with me in pure Brahminical Tamil because he recognized me as a Brahmin.

Where are Christians who can speak in languages familiar to the people? If a new believer ever goes to a church service, he cannot even understand the message, not to mention all the other activities of the church. If he wants to survive among them, then he must become conformed to their image in all the areas of his life. But the church will remain Westernized and will not be bothered about either the new believers or the common people yet to be reached with the gospel.

Why do we stand and preach like a politician while conducting *satsanghs* or night meetings or even television programs? Even on the mission field during services and gospel meetings, it is always better to sit and preach. Once when I asked people to remove the table and chair and arrange a cot (*chowki*) for me to sit on and preach, a missionary could not understand and even raised his objection by saying, "This is the way we are used to preaching and would you please do likewise. This will help us to see the people properly." But I compelled him to make the arrangement as I requested. Though he was murmuring, at the end of the meeting he said, "You are right. It not only gave a nice look, but you also conducted the *satsangh* as they (Hindus) usually do." During l992, at YCLT in Yavatmal, I even asked them to remove the pulpit, and I sat and preached in the chapel service, which was welcomed by many.

Not only should we sit and preach, but as much as possible, we must wear traditional Indian clothing. I cannot understand why most convention speakers (with rare exceptions) use only Western dress, especially a tie. Particularly on the mission field, we should not allow speakers to use Western dress, specifically a tie. Let them keep it inside their churches. (For those who argue that even Indians, as in television newsreaders, are wearing ties, so why should we not wear them also, it should be enough to say that newsreaders are not accused of being agents of foreign propaganda, as Christian evangelists invariably are.)

We must face the possibility that our failure to communicate clearly, simply and understandably reveals deep problems within ourselves. As James H. Jauncey has written in *Above Ourselves:*

> Christian love for the listener will also prevent us from using speech or conversation to show off superior knowledge, which may be beyond the comprehension of the listener. As a rule, what we cannot put into simple language, we do not really understand ourselves.[1]

In considering the level of understanding of the people we seek to reach, we must think in terms of the whole person (if not the whole society) and not just the mental faculties. "Total man needs the total gospel." Man is basically a person, a human being, and not merely a thing. Thus in all our efforts to communicate the gospel to our neighbor, we must approach him as a person.

Perhaps our biggest failure in communicating our message is that we have mechanized it. Technology has come to dominate personality, as we churn out tons of literature and produce films, radio and television programs. But the personal touch, the essence of biblical communication, is neglected if not lost. At the personal level, we can touch every person if we move with patience rather than with big programs.

Every person is striving to achieve some kind of fulfillment in all walks of life. This longing for fulfillment reveals the lack of perfection or satisfaction in the life that he is living. Though one feels satisfied in one area of his life, his natural desire for total or complete perfection in other areas of his life will always force him to search for it. This shows the complexity of the human personality. The fullness of the human personality includes physical, mental, moral, social and spiritual aspects. Even though we cannot limit human life to just these areas, generally they are the areas in which we all strive to achieve perfection. Likewise, we cannot put these parts of life in watertight compartments. As the human psyche is complex, human life is also complex, and one area depends on the others.

Each family and society is made up of people with these varying and complex personalities. What gives satisfaction to one need not give the same to the other. For this reason, we cannot have a uniform theory or policy in all of our approaches to reach these varied and complex people. This being the truth, in all our efforts to reach our neighbor, proper preparation is needed on our part to first understand them. Though basic human needs in life are almost the same, yet they differ in degree (not necessarily in kind), according to different personalities, so we cannot use the same approach for all.

One cannot simply understand another's worldview based on his own personal experience in life. Subsequently, to gain understanding of another's view, one must first win his confidence. Then alone, will he trust you to some extent and will share his views with you, both by words and deeds, and will perhaps even approach you for the fulfillment in his life. For all of this, you must step into his shoes.

Winning another's confidence, particularly our neighbor's, is not an easy thing. A person will put his trust in someone only when he is sure that the person is truly interested in his life. The problem in most Christian evangelism is that there is no patience to win the confidence of our neighbor. With a wrong interpretation of the philosophy of "win the winnable while they are winnable," we do not have time for love and concern and friendship. *If our neighbor is not a prosperous candidate for quick baptism, then we too do not have time for him in our proselytizing efforts.* And in this way, we are more concerned to fulfill our evangelistic desire than to help our neighbor to find fulfillment in his life. By this, we are using our neighbor to satisfy our ego, and using people to satisfy one's own ego is not only a crime but also a sin against God because we are despising the very work of God, who created man in His own image.

To win others' confidence is not easy, because Christians do not have a very good reputation for friendliness with people of other religions. Our haste to evangelize can offend and reinforce the idea that Christians are only proselytizers who do not truly care for people. It is wrong to approach a neighbor with the hidden motive of converting him. Even a fool will soon realize the true motive. Rather, prepare yourself to be spent in the task of friendship and love. When one seriously desires to reach a neighbor, there is an accompanying moral responsibility to invest his life in that task. "The greater the privilege, the greater the responsibility." Don't run ahead of God, but be faithful and sincere and alert for the proper opportunity to speak of Christ; leave the remainder in God's hand. "God won't do your part and God's part you cannot do."

B. IN OUR WORSHIP

Worship is the pivot on which the entire spiritual life revolves, particularly for Hindus. They never worship just three hours in a week plus (bonus) one house prayer meeting. "Hinduism is not a Sunday church devotion or a Friday mosque religion." [2] After more than a decade as a *bhakta* of Christ (and surviving with Christians to some extent), I can hardly even join in the worship at a Christian Sunday church service. Here is one living example: In a conference, the music team "led" us in what they called true worship, but I could hardly join with them. Even for the few songs they sang in Indian languages, there was either Western or Westernized "light" music. While there, I often dreamed in this way—remove all the Western musical instruments, and also even the pulpit; spread a dari (thick carpet) on the stage, have one *bhajan* team lead in singing beautiful *bhajans* (traditional, Indian devotional songs); then, how we could all worship the Lord in spirit and truth!

This does not mean that the music team failed to lead us to worship in spirit and truth, nor that none of us worshipped in spirit and truth. I saw that others really worshipped the Lord, even dancing. ("Walk, walk, walk, walking with the Lord.") But I could not join with them in it. "In a group, we cannot look after each and every individual's interest," would be a convincing answer. But remember that I am sharing this not as an isolated individual, but representing the whole mass of new converts whom they are trying to mold according to the Christian image. Rev. John Stott, an authoritative evangelical scholar, calls this proselytizing:

> To proselytize is to convert somebody else to our opinions and culture, and to squeeze him into our mold; to evangelize is to proclaim God's good news about Jesus to the end that people will believe Him, find life in Him and ultimately be conformed to His image, not ours.[3]

Try taking one pure, pakka (first–rate) Indian *bhajan* team to England or America, and ask them to lead the church congregation in worship, singing English songs in Indian *bhajan* tunes. What would the response be? Out of curiosity, they may enjoy the funny songs, but they will never feel like they are worshipping. (Better first try it here in English services before going to America or England.)

This is not my experience alone. Fr. W. Lash of Christa Seva Sangha Ashram shares the following experience about a Brahmin teacher who served in the mission:

> He [the teacher] had a great admiration for all that the missionaries were doing–schools, hospitals, and social work among the poor. Then he added, "They must believe Jesus to be a very fine man because they follow his example very carefully. But I do not think they believe He is God." I was greatly startled, and asked him what had brought him to conclude this. He answered, "They do not worship him."...It had not been apparent to this thoughtful Brahmin, who had seen the life of the mission day by day. There had been nothing in it which corresponded to his ideas of worship. That brought to me very forcibly the fact that often without our knowing it, the very basis of our life and work may be missed because it is not revealed in a form which those around us can really understand.[4]

Music is an integral part of worship in the Hindu community. Several times they have *naadopasana* (music worship) alone. But even living in this country with rich classical music (both Carnatic and Hindustani), the churches have sadly preferred to adopt Western music for their worship. By saying this, I am not degrading Western music. Let the Westerners have their own music, but why should we abandon God's rich gift to us in Indian music?

Even in the church today, the only "official" musical instrument is the organ, and in every Christian home, boys and girls are learning only the guitar. Even those beautiful lyrics composed in earlier times in India have now become light music in the church. To top it all, nowadays disco and rock music have become the norm, even in worship, and are used in evangelistic camps.

The usual response to this is "Even Hindus learn and use the guitar and enjoy disco music." But while a Hindu may use Western music in the cinema and enjoy disco music in a party, he would certainly not use them in his *bhajan mandalis* and *satsanghs*. Even though our people have started leaning towards modern Western trends, it is our responsibility to help preserve the cultural heritage of this nation. Even apart from this, there is need for caution. I must now say what some people keep saying to me. Contextualization is not compromise, nor conforming to the image of the world, but rather it is allowing the gospel to become incarnate in the existing culture in faithfulness to the Bible. Rock and disco music may be popular in the modern world, but because they are largely related to sensation and erotic feelings, we must be careful in using them in both worship and ministry.

When I ask the Christians why we should use hymns with Western music rather than compose and use *bhajans,* their reaction generally is, "Oh, we don't want to sing *bhajans* like the Hindus, we want to have our own Christian music." For them, Western music itself is Christian music, and they do not even know that the so–called Christian (Western) music has heathen ancestry. There exists no Christian music or Christian culture. Wherever the gospel went, except in India (to speak an oversimplified generalization), it adopted and adapted the existing culture to give its expression within it. But only in India, particularly in Christian circles, everything Western becomes Christian and everything Indian becomes pagan.

My Norwegian friend Ramslien, who served seven years in Pakistan as a missionary, once said to me, "When I was in Pakistan, sometimes I worshipped in Pakistani churches, but since I came to India, I worship only in Western churches." In Delhi, there is a church in a theatre with air–conditioning and push back seats. The one excuse for them to keep that theatre is to comfortably accommodate the foreigners who used to go there for the service. But the same foreigners, when they visit the Hindu *ashrams,* walk barefoot, sit on the floor and even eat vegetarian food. Even Prince Charles of England and the late Princess Diana walked barefoot at Gandhi's *samadhi* in Delhi during their visit to India. But we have more excuses for why we cannot do a thing than reasons why we ought to do it.

When I was in a Christian ashram (where they still eat food on the dining table and use non–vegetarian food regularly, degrading the very concept of *ashram* in India), once a group of more than fifty Hindus came to visit. The then acharya received them in the drawing room. After some talk, he shared something about the ashram, and then the Christian ashramites sang one or two hymns (not *bhajans*), sitting on the easy chairs. After the hymns, the leader of the visiting group wanted to sing some *bhajan* and the acharya gave permission. However, before they started to sing, all those who were sitting on the chairs (of course not the ashramites) came down to the floor and sat along with the others to join in the *bhajan*. Only Christians, not only in the churches but even in house meetings, will sit on easy chairs (that too with crossed legs) to worship the Lord (and definitely with shoes on).

To win the hearts and minds of our people towards the Lord, our way of worshipping should not only be attractive but should also create respect and reverence in their minds. Otherwise, they will not have the regard for our way of worship that they feel for their own. As they sit hour after hour on the floor for meditation and worship, when they see us sitting comfortably on a chair or sofa, it does not create a good impression in their sprit. Inevitably, people of other faiths will think and do think that they know how to worship and respect God and consider that their ways of worship are the best ones; and our actions confirm this in their minds every time they see our strange habits.

The counter argument for all this is "Oh, God sees only the heart not where you sit and what you put on. Even the Hindus are wearing jeans when they go the temple, so why object to us alone?" A Hindu may go to the temple with jeans, but will never enter it with shoes and sit on an easy chair to worship God. Some full–time mission workers on the field, will even read the Bible in the morning without washing their face and mouth, even sitting on the very bed in which they slept, which is an abomination unthinkable to the Hindus. God does not mind our dress and mannerisms, but people do.

Yet, for every point along these lines, there is a counterpoint. We are not ready to understand the feelings of others in these areas. That is why Christianity cannot make any impact on the hearts and minds of Hindus. It is not hard to understand the problem of Christians who are born and brought up in a Westernized Christian sub–culture. (One brother said to me, "I feel like worshipping only when I hear organ music and singing three "amens" at the end.") One must be sensitive not to deny anyone the right to worship the Lord in any way, but my plea is that we do not impose Western music on the new believers as the only real Christian music and worship. Even in tribal areas, the (south) Indian missionaries introduce Western music and forms of worship, rather than following tribal (Indian) forms.

To understand the greatness of Indian music, just attend any music program or watch one on television (either *Carnatic* or *Hindustani*) and see how the singer sings numerous songs for not less than three hours without ever seeing any music notes or songbook. For most of the Christian music with Western notes, you cannot sing without the aid of books. To my surprise, I saw that Christians, even missionaries, could not sing more than two or three songs without seeing a book. On the other hand, Hindus sing *bhajan* after *bhajan* from their heart without seeing a book. Such is the richness of Indian music, which we Hindus do not want to exchange for rock and disco.

The response of a senior missionary was "When we use a guitar and drum people gather, but if we use a *harmonium* and *tabla* who will gather?" But he forgot that *tamasas* (circuses) always attract, but only for their own sake. People may pay attention to the musical instruments but will not pay attention to the meaning of the song, nor can they join in the singing. But while singing *bhajans,* they immediately pick up both the tune and words and join in singing.

I confess with much pain, that I never feel like worshipping in any church in India, irrespective of the denomination. (I rarely attended church services, and that was only on invitation to preach, which I have completely stopped now). There has long been a cry, and several attempts have been made to make the church worship in an indigenous way, and the story of these failed attempts will not be recounted here. But one point must be made. Just sitting on the floor and using a few Indian musical instruments will not make worship indigenous. Several things have to be radically changed. In this area, the Roman Catholics, particularly their *ashrams,* went ahead of everyone to the other extreme of making Christianity as another cult within Hinduism.

I hear your immediate response: "That is why we want to keep a different identity. It is better to follow Western methods to keep the identity separate than to make Christianity another cult within Hinduism." This is the modern inquisition in Protestant (especially evangelical) circles. *In order to save the body they want to kill the very soul.*

All is not lost because someone and something has gone wrong. In every new endeavor, there is always an initial risk to be taken, which can later be corrected. Over caution is equally as dangerous as over enthusiasm. The former with research and analysis will kill the very spirit of the new endeavor, and the latter will end up in compromise and confusion.

Another objection to indigenous worship forms is the objection raised by the Hindu fundamentalists against the "adopting and adapting" of Hindu dharma by Christians (particularly Catholic ashrams) in order to present Christianity as an indigenous faith ("disguised in Hindu forms," to use Sita Ram Goel's description[5]):

> "The Indianization of Christianity is a serious matter" as the mission is "casting a covetous glance before mounting a marauding expedition. What causes concern is the future of the Hindu culture once it falls into the hands of the church. The fate of Greek culture after it was taken over by the Church is a grim reminder."

> As the mission under "imperialist enterprise" failed to "make the strides it should have made by virtue of its own merits and the opportunities that came its way," now there is the latest method called "indigenization" which "sounds soft but is no less sinister" as it is nothing else but "it is evangelization. It is the planting of the gospel inside another culture, another philosophy, another religion." In fact, the call from the resurgent Hindu leaders is to oppose it as both Hindu religion and culture–which according to them are inseparable–are at stake.

The call is given considering three main reasons:

1   Under the disguise of indigenization they (mostly Catholics) have no right to selectively embrace "those parts of

Hindu spiritual discipline and culture which they find inspiring."

2   "The whole business could have been dismissed with the contempt it deserves or laughed out as ludicrous but for the massive finance and the giant apparatus which the Christian mission in India has at its disposal."

3   And, "many Hindus, raised on decades of uncritical acceptance of any form of religious expression, may simply not care one way or the other," and thereby, they are not aware of the facts that "a well monied and successful missionary is regarded as a threat to the National stability." [6]

Well, if we accept all their objections (some of which are true) and stop any effort towards indigenization, then we have to stop even preaching the gospel, as they object to the spread of the gospel in India under any form. If we cannot stop preaching the gospel because of other's objections, then why should we stop indigenization for the same reasons? To make the church relevant to our context, a lot of radical changes have to be made, as in church architecture, pastors' dress, pulpit, altar, the way we celebrate communion service, music, theology, even church administration, etc. (One must conclude that this level of change is never going to happen in the existing churches in India—this is neither pessimism nor prophecy but a down–to–earth reality.)

Most Christians are born and brought up in the Indian "Christian" sub–culture and so cannot understand the extent to which they are following Western methods in worshipping, witnessing, church administration, etc. Some new converts are virtually brainwashed and become worse than the traditional Christians, more Westernized than the Westernized Indian Christians. Of course the Western culture and modernism give a lot of comforts to the body. Without understanding their "plight" and our struggle to survive as *bhaktas* of Christ in India, some such simply write:

> Their doctrine is to bring Christianity in Indian culture. In India there exists nearly 2,000 castes and cultures. And to which culture will they change Christianity? In Indian culture generally, the priests used to be naked above the waist with kudumi (sacred tuft of hair). Can those CSI pastors or the bishops who support such an Indianization change themselves in

such a way? By replacing candles to oil lamps (kutuvilakku), what spiritual change do they expect? What is the problem in the Western way of worship? As spiritual life is not important for them, they try to bring these revolutionary changes.[7]

Perhaps this is written against church fads, often initiated from the west like our present irrelevant forms. But in asking what problem is present in Western worship, the writer shows that he has never listened, and so never cared to listen, to Hindu perceptions of Christianity and Christian expressions in India. Though some Indian Christians are strongly patronizing Western worship, thankfully several Western Christians agree with us:

Regulations concerning the ministry, liturgies, customs, hymns, and traditions are often only Western cultural transplants, which grow poorly among people of another culture....

Most worship services in non—Western cultures still follow liturgies that grew up in Western civilization. If people from other cultural backgrounds learn to love and appreciate these traditions, this should be applauded. However, if through church control, denominations discourage innovation and spontaneity in worship, they kill the spirit.

Today the church needs the grace to "let go." Cannot the Holy Spirit lead in matters of liturgy and worship? Furthermore, if this can be done in Western congregations, why cannot it be done in non—Western cultures? Mistakes will be made. These are inevitable. Yet, the corrections to be made should be done by the Christians in that culture rather than by "seminary—trained" officials who might not even understand what they are condemning and controlling.[8]

There may be thousands of genuine reasons to follow a Western way of worship in Indian churches, but we have a yet stronger reason to adopt indigenous forms: we are Indians and we are biblical. Milk may be rich and liquid, yet fish cannot survive in it. We would prefer to survive in our own water, of course removing the unbiblical scum from it.

C. In Our Language

"Would you please read the following verses?" I requested of a young man before beginning to share the message in a worship service. Though Srinivasan, a Tamil Brahmin, started off enthusiastically, it was only with much difficulty that he managed to read through the five verses. He found the language not only irrelevant but also uncommunicative. His is not an isolated case. I myself faced the same problem in the early years after I become a Yesu *bhakta*. Not only the language, but also the way it has been written, hardly communicates to a follower of another faith who, for the first time, begins reading the Bible.

In most major languages, the Bible is only available in a style that is outmoded. This is another factor that impedes effective communication. New translations are coming out but are hardly encouraged. Anyone working among a particular group of people must endeavor to produce literature in their own heart language.

Just give a Bible (particularly in any Dravidian language) to any one, and ask him if he understands the message. For most people, understanding the language of the Bible is impossible in one reading. In my early days as a *bhakta* of Jesus, several times I asked the missionary to translate verses from biblical Tamil to common Tamil (now I have become familiar with it, thanks to "Christian" influence). Those who know English can understand the message more clearly by reading the new English translations than by reading in their own heart Indian language.

Of course a great many Indian Christians, particularly among the evangelicals, will not understand this, as they are accustomed to reading their daily devotion in their heavenly language called English. Reading the Bible in an Indian language is perhaps less dignified; this probably contributes to the lack of understanding of the common peoples' problem.

The usual defense on this point is "The gospel is a mystery and one cannot easily understand it, however simple the language may be." And further, "Those who have responded to the gospel so far, responded not because of the language, but because of the message they got; and however simple the language, until God reveals Himself, nobody can understand the Bible. Above all, with all its limitation and mistakes, if you and several others came to know the Lord only through the existing translation, why do you now demand a new one? So if God wants to save a person, the translation is not a problem. However simple the translation may be, unless one explains it, a person cannot understand it. Thus, it is better to explain the present translation and encourage him to read it. Those who translated the Bible were no fools, and with much prayer alone, they have done it. And as God has *inspired their translation* why should we change it?" But if, instead of accepting our mistakes, we take refuge in the doctrines of God's election and predestination, then where does the necessity of even preaching the gospel come at all?

In no other department of Christian ministry is so much money and energy invested without proper results, as in the field of literature. Here as in all areas, we must follow the example of Christ. Jesus used the common language of His day (Aramaic) to share His message. Yet, I have seen in Tamil Nadu a Tamil preacher preaching in English to a Tamil audience, with interpretation from English to Tamil! I witnessed this twice, in Nagercoil and in Trichy.[9] The disciples of Christ used what is called koine Greek, which was the bazaar language of their day. They never used classical Greek, although some New Testament writings are in a more "cultured" style than others. But we are using as well as giving others age–old translations, which are not communicating the message.

One day in a class with more than 20 Tamil missionaries, I asked the meaning of one particular word in Matt. 23:23 (ottalam in Tamil). To my surprise, none of them could give the meaning for it. Though they can be excused, as most of them are using only English Bibles, yet all of them were well aware that such a word is there. Some of them were theological graduates and most of them traditional Christians. After giving the meaning, I pointed out similar other words in the Old and New Testaments and said, "All these years, you are using and reading the Bible without even knowing the meaning of the words." The only response was silence. The most surprising thing in this situation is that those Tamils who oppose any new Tamil translation of the Bible, do not know the fact that the present Tamil Bible which they are using is itself a revision and not the original translation done by earlier missionaries.

Though new translations are coming in major languages, they are not encouraged by people in the church. After a long search, I got a copy of one for myself in Tamil (as I still read the Bible only in my own heavenly language of Tamil, or in our national language, Hindi). When I shared this need, one evangelical leader said, "If they are not even allowing us to change the color on the edge of the paper (gold or red), then where does the question of a new translation come?" Thankfully, some Christian leaders strongly recommend the need for proper new translations in Tamil.

Lack of true concern to communicate the gospel is the main reason for this. In this business–oriented world, Christians are merely selling some information about the gospel to the people in the name of literature ministry. Tons and tons of literature are being distributed without much result. Probably not even 5% of the missionaries read the tracts before they distribute them to other people. Above all, their aim is only to complete certain annual targets. They forget the fact that new translations and new literature are needed, not only to share the gospel to others, but also to strengthen the faith of new believers. Both in outreach and follow up ministry, the same kind of literature is used.

Here is a challenge. Take one particular area, in which lots of literature has been distributed for a period of six months. Then take a survey of the whole area, collecting statistics of how many people even read the literature completely, how many of those who read understood the message and how many finally made any surrender to Christ. Do not say that still, irrespective of all the shortcomings we all know this would reveal, people are coming to Christ through literature ministry. Because of God's grace, they may come to Christ, not because of, but in spite of our efforts.

Another problem is the distribution of Bibles and New Testaments to people in the name of mass evangelism. If some Hindus give the Gita or Veda to lay Christians, will they understand anything out of it? I was shocked when I came to know that the book *Hundred Bible Lessons* was being sold to Hindus after open air preaching. When I raised an objection, the only reply was "Push as much biblical literature as possible into the hands of the people is our slogan." What kind of logic is there in distributing such books or even Bibles and New Testaments to the common Hindus who cannot understand anything in them? Particularly when a Hindu opens the Hindi New Testament, on the first page, he reads (Matthew chapter one) nothing but Muslim names and throws away the book. Why does the Bible Society of India not print the Bible and New Testament in Hindi, keeping the Gospel of John first instead of Matthew? I have been told that, at one time, the Hindi New Testament was published with Mark's gospel.

I have raised my doubts about literature ministry several times with a few of those who are involved, but always received some kind of negative answer. They criticize me that I neither understand Christianity nor the ministry. But what kind of answer will they will give to D. Martyn Lloyd Jones who raised the same issue? He wrote:

> Lastly, there is a question which we might ask here. And I deliberately put it in the form of a question because I admit quite frankly that I am not quite clear in my own mind what the answer should be. Is there, I wonder, a query, a question, perhaps a warning, in this verse (Matt. 7:6) regarding the indiscriminate distribution of the Scriptures? I am simply raising a question for you to consider and for you to discuss with others. If I am told that I have to discriminate in speaking to people about these things, if I have to differentiate between type and type and person and person, and about the particular truth I give to each, is it a good thing to put the whole Bible within the reach of people who can be described as spiritual dogs and swine? May it not sometimes lead to blasphemy and cursing and to behavior and conduct of swinish character? Is it always right, I wonder, to put certain texts of Scripture on placards, especially those referring to the blood of Christ? I have often, myself, heard those very things leading to blasphemy. I simply put the questions. Think of the eunuch in Acts viii going back from Jerusalem. He had his Scriptures and was actually reading them, when Philip approached him and said: "Understandest thou what thou readest?" And he replied, "How can I, except some man should guide me?" Exposition is generally necessary, and you cannot do away with the human instrument as a general rule.

> "But," we protest, "look at the wonderful effect of the distribution of the Scriptures." If we could discover the exact facts, I wonder how many people we should find who have been converted apart from human agency? I know there are wonderful, exceptional cases. I have read stories of people

who have been converted in that way. Thank God that kind of thing can happen. But I suggest that it is not the normal method. Does not the fact that we have to be careful in our choice of aspects of truth as we deal with different people raise a query in our minds? Sometimes, of course, we try to avoid the duty of speaking, by giving a Gospel or Scripture portion, but that is not God's normal way. The way of God has always been the presenting of the truth immediately through personality, man expounding the Scriptures. If you have a conversation with a man and are able to point out the truth to him, he may then ask for a copy of the Scriptures, or you may feel you should give him one. That is right and good. Give him your Scripture. The query I am raising has reference to the indiscriminate placing of the Bible where there is no one to explain it, and where a man, in the condition described by our Lord in the verse of our text (Matt.7: 6), is facing this great and mighty truth without a human guide.

This probably comes as a surprise to many, but I suggest that we need to think again carefully about some of these matters. We become slaves to custom and to certain habits and practices, and very often we become quite unscriptural as we do so. I thank God that we have this great written Word of God; but I have often felt that it would not be a bad thing to experiment for a while with the idea of not allowing anybody to have a copy of the Scriptures unless he showed signs of spiritual life. That may be going too far, but I have felt sometimes that doing this would impress upon people the precious nature of this Book, its wonderful character, and the privilege of being allowed to possess it and to read it. It might not only be a good thing for the souls of those who are outside; it would certainly give the Church a completely new conception of this priceless treasure that God has put into our hands."

Further on this point, either consciously or unconsciously we use a lot of technical terms, some of which are merely ineffective and others of which are actually offensive. Words like conversion, crusade, mission and missionary have become offensive in our communal society. Terms like baptism, amen, *padri,* pastor, Christian (*Isayee, masihi*), etc., do not communicate anything near an appropriate meaning. There are proper Indian terms which can be used instead of each of these.

Besides, if we want to get a good response among the Hindus, we must freely and liberally use Indian terms. Of course, there are certain terms, which may be totally unbiblical and may even lead to compromise in our doctrines. This we will discuss elsewhere. Till then, let us remember that, to communicate the gospel, we must use the people's language not the pulpit one.

There are many beautiful Indian terms that somehow have become taboo among Christians. For example, *bhagavan* is a beautiful word meaning "blessed one." Why do we not use it? Some say *bhagavan* is not for the supreme God but only for an *avatar* like Rama and Krishna, and therefore, we should not use it for our Lord. Where this interpretation came from, I don't know![12] If we can say "O blessed Lord" while praying in English, why not use *bhagavan* while praying in Hindi (or any other Indian language)? For this, the answer is that by using such Hindu terms, we are equating our Lord with their gods. But then, what about the word prabhu (Lord) that we are using? Even in the Old Testament, that word is used for kings and husbands. Are we equating God with kings and husbands?

By not using such an Indian term are we really conveying to the non–Christians that we are worshipping a higher or greater God than they worship? To an average (even educated) Hindu, we are worshipping a different God but not a higher or better God than they worship. For them, Muslims worship *Allah* or *Khuda,* Hindus worship *bhagavan* or *Iswar* and Christians worship "God." For them, "God" that we worship is not a greater God than what they call as *Brahman,* nor even an English word, but it is the name of the Christian *bhagavan* (like Yahweh, the proper name of God in the Old Testament). When I was in Madhubani in North Bihar, Veerendra Misra used to say, "*Swamiji aap hamaare liye gaad* (not God) *se praartanaa keejiye*"; which is "you please pray to *gaad* [here it stands for the proper name of the Christian *bhagavan*] for us."

When I was sharing this and recommending another word, *Sri,* as in *Sri Khrist Bhagavan, Sri Khrist bhakta mandali,* etc., one senior missionary objected to it by saying, "By using 'Sri' we are equating our Lord with human beings, as the Hindus use this to address others as Sri Yogesh Patel, etc. And since Sri is used by the Hindus to give respect to human beings as well as to their gods like Sri Ram, Sri Sankar Bhagavan, etc., we cannot use it for our Lord." For this, I brought to his kind attention the word "Lord," which is used for kings and husbands in the Old Testament. Sarah called Abraham as lord. Of course, as Christians are always using "Mr." or "Bro.," they cannot understand this. These are just examples of our rejecting Indian terms by giving them our own interpretation and rejecting them as Hindu terms. (But with surprising inconsistency, most of these forbidden terms are sung in lyrics in the various languages, as poets have more sense than theologians do. For example, in Tamil lyrics, Hindu terms like mangalam are used, and there is even a mangalam *bhajan* for Jesus composed by Vedanayagam Sastriyar.[13])

"Instead of borrowing or using 'Hindu' (Indian) words and terms, coin your own new words," suggested one person. But our aim is to communicate and not to create another modern language. Already we have "biblical" languages and "pulpit" terms. And coining such new terms would not serve our purpose; the new words would have to be explained in common language, which people can understand.

For holy communion, we use strange words like *prabhu bhoj* or *raa bhoj* (Hindi); or *narkarunai, tiruvirundu* (Tamil), etc. But for this, we can use the Indian word *prasad,* which means "grace." But all Christians are united (at least in this) in objection by saying, "If we use the word prasad, the Hindus and new believers may think that we are distributing *prasad,* as they distribute in the Hindu temples." But are we not receiving God's grace through the elements served during the communion service? When we need to explain to every new believer what is meant by strange words such as *sakiramandu* (used by Tamil Protestants) or *paska bali* (the Roman Catholic term) for communion service, why not give the same explanation and use the Indian word *prasad* (prasadam in Tamil)?

In the area of literature, a thorough revolution ought to be made. Most Scriptures in India are written in poetic form, which makes them easy for memorization and meditation. We need to make efforts to present the gospel message in such a form. I would rather suggest that we go a step further and render the New Testament in poetry. *Nayaa Kaavya,* a version of the four gospels in Hindi verse by S. K. Peter (from the ISPCK,

Delhi) is encouraging. This would go a long way in helping even the illiterate to remember God's word. The *Sri Khrist Gita* by Dhanjibhai Fakirbhai was a positive step in this direction, but the book has been unavailable for decades. Recently, a "Sermon On The Mount In Verse" (*Parvatiiya Pravachan*) written in the famous poetic meter of *chowpai,* like that of the Tulsi Ramayana, by Prabhu Dat Mishra in 1958, was uncovered from layers of dust in a theological library. Can we not at least feel ashamed of these things?

Jesus was completely oriental in His method of teaching. He followed the Oriental's method of oral tradition by using poetical devices which would help His disciples to remember His words, verbatim (e.g. Mk. 8:35; Lk. 6:43). As already mentioned, we must follow the footsteps of the apostles in using the common language of the people to present the gospel both in our message and literature. Specific literature must be produced to cater to the needs of a particular group. Anyone who is born and brought up with a particular Bible translation may feel uncomfortable with the modern translations that are coming in the Indian vernaculars. But when we welcome RSV, NIV, and Good News Bibles, why hesitate with translations in Indian languages only? And those who know a little English are going to use only the English Bible for their devotions and never the Bible in their heart language (irrespective of all the shortcomings in it), so why should they object to others using new translations?

At least in printing Christian literature other than the Bible, we must use the common language of the people. For this, we must read a lot of secular magazines to know the trend of the current language of the people. Even in tracts, we are using Bible verses as they are in the old language. Surely, here at least, change can be made. This now seems to be a universally recognized truth, as summarized by John Stott:

> ...[concerning] those social customs which form the background of some biblical instruction [but] are entirely foreign to those of our day....accept the biblical instruction itself as permanently binding....But to translate it into contemporary cultural terms...it is essential to recognize that the purpose of "cultural transposition" (the practice of transposing the teaching

of the Scripture from one culture into another) is not to avoid obedience
but rather to ensure it, by making it contemporary....To be concerned only
with the ancient text and ignore its modern application is antiquarianism;
to search for a living message without first wrestling with the original
meaning is existentialism..."[14]

Some specific terminological changes, which can be made to
assist communication with Hindus, are:

diksha instead of baptism
acharya instead of pastor or padri
mandir instead of girija or church
Khristabhakta or *Yesu bhakta* instead of *Masihi* or *Isaayi*
Sri Khrist bhakta mandali instead of local church
Khrist–Yesu panth instead of Christianity or *Isai Dharm*
prasad instead of communion
dharmikta instead of *dharm*
Jesus jayanti instead of Christmas
tatastu instead of amen

We recommend these new terms out of our personal experience in ministry in the north. At the same time, it can never be
insisted on that these terms should be uniformly followed everywhere. Each language and social group may have different but
specific local terms, and they must be properly studied first and
used, particularly replacing Greek, Aramaic and Western terms
like baptism, amen, pastor, etc.

While they use Sanskrit terms in Tamil and other Dravidian languages like *jnanasnanam, jnanadeekshai* for baptism,
why should they object to use of the word *diksha* in Hindi for
the same? When we say to the people, particularly to high caste
contacts, that they should take "baptism" to confess their faith in
Christ, they get scared. Generally "baptism" creates a very wrong
understanding in that it not only denotes a change in religious allegiance but also the abandoning of Hindu culture and society for
a Western religion and culture. Particularly caste Hindus think
that during baptism, the *padri* (pastor) will immerse the candidate
in the water and will push a small peace of beef (particularly that
of cow) into his mouth in order to make him a *Isaayi* (Christian).
Whereas, when we say that they should take *diksha* (guru diksha)
to confess their faith in Christ, they clearly understand and usually no objection comes from the family either.

Similarly, because the Muslims are also using Amin in their prayers, Hindus hesitate to join with us to say the same. However, when we use tatastu (which means "let it be so" or "amen," just translating into Sanskrit, which in theory everyone must approve) even without inviting them, they join with us to say it after our prayers. I witnessed this in several places in the north. In Rajastan at Hanumanagarh, the minibus driver who used to come daily and take us for *satsangh* meetings joined with us to say *tatastu* when we were praying before we left for the meeting, without being invited. The same driver previously used to stand outside and never joined with us when we used "amen."

In reference to this, one Tamil brother said, "We can use *tatastu* in the north, but what about in the south?" "Coin your own Tamil word or use 'amen' as it is" is my answer to that. But most caste Hindus, and particularly Brahmins, in the south also understand *tatastu* (this does not mean that everything that we attempt in contextualization is to accommodate the Brahminical system or culture). My friend in Bangalore endorsed that even *Vaisya* (business caste) community people in Karnataka use this word.

The common complaint raised by several Christians against me is "Because you are a Brahmin, you want to change everything according to your Brahminical tradition." One Church of North India pastor even said to me, "Indianization means Sanskritization, Sanskritization means Brahminization, which is nothing but 'Hindu Imperialism' and that is why we oppose it, as Brahmins again want to impose their cultural and religious tradition on us by back door ways." A missionary, similarly, commented "This is the one area which you Brahmins have left so far. Now you all started to get converted and try to dominate the church and mission as you are dominating the Hindu society up to this day."

However, this ignores the fact that I am not imposing my ideas on others, and I never expect others to follow blindly. My intention is not to give a uniform formula to be applied everywhere. I share some principles, and if it is relevant to your context, use it or leave it. But please, be careful that while opposing such "Hindu or Brahminical imperialism" you do not continue to impose on converts a continuance of your own "Western imperialism" which is inherited in all the churches. Without knowing the cultural, social and religious life of the people among whom they serve, missionaries and evangelists simply impose their own traditions on new believers. They want to use the down south drum in north Bihar instead of using the local musical instruments. Yet, even when I point this out, they call it Hindu imperialism imposed in the name of indigenization!

Though from the beginning of this century several attempts were made by missionaries like Dr. E. Stanley Jones to separate Christ from Western Christianity, their Indian successors did not carry out their vision. As most of the Hindus, including the educated ones, always relate Christianity with Western civilization, most of the Christian terms and traditions are also viewed in the same way. Paul Martin, in his book on Stanley Jones, analyzing Jones' "Distinction between Christ and Christianity" (pp.77–115) and says "Jones was convinced that the figure of Jesus taken straight from the Gospels was enough to draw Indians to Christ. What we needed was to prevent Christ from being obscured by the West, by the Church, or by Christianity itself." [15]

But where are such missionaries of "the Indian road" today, and why were their insights never heeded by the church? Unteachability is the greatest crime.

D. IN OUR THEOLOGY

Some of my very good friends, who seek to understand and support me, on reading this manuscript confessed that they did not really know what Indian theology and Western theology meant. (To my surprise, even one who had studied 18 months in a Bible Institute (BBI). When educated and well informed Christians confess this, it shows again how comfortable Indian Christians are in their traditions, and how they fail to understand a Hindu perspective on their churches and their "Christian religion.") I do not think a better brief summary of

Western theology and the need for change can be given than
this from the "Seoul Declaration":

> Western theology is, by and large rationalistic, molded by Western phi-
> losophies, preoccupied with intellectual concerns, especially those having
> to do with faith and reason. All too often, it has reduced the Christian
> faith to abstract concepts which may have answered the questions of the
> past, but which fail to grapple with the issues of today. It has consciously
> been conformed to the secularistic worldview associated with the enlight-
> enment....Furthermore, having been wrought in Christendom, it hardly
> addresses the questions of people living in situations characterized by re-
> ligious pluralism, secularism, resurgent Islam, or Marxist totalitarianism...
> .Consequently, we insist on the need for critical reflection and theological
> renewal. We urgently need an Evangelical theology, which is faithful to
> Scripture and relevant to the varied situations in the third world.[16]

What people of other faiths see in India is only a Western
church, not just in structure and worship but also in theology and doctrine. India is a country where *anubhava* holds the
pramaana (experience holds the evidence, see note 51 of the
previous chapter), while in most churches what is presented
is a rational religion which is pulpit centered. A truly Indian
Christian theology is not encouraged by Indian Christians, and
particularly evangelicals seem paralyzed by a fear of syncretism.
While endeavoring to formulate any theology and doctrine that
would be relevant to a particular group, we must make a mar-
ginal allowance for mistakes, which could be later corrected.
R. D. Immanuel points out that the story of the early church's
formulation of its Christology shows that its stand, on such an
important aspect of theology, was revised more than four times:

> The Council of Nicea (325 A. D.) declares that Jesus Christ is truly God. The
> Council of Constantinople (381 A. D.) declares that Jesus Christ is truly hu-
> man. The Council of Ephesus (431 A. D.) declares that Jesus Christ is both
> God and man in one Person.The Council of Chalcedon (451 A. D.) declares
> that the One Lord, Jesus Christ, is both God and man.[17]

Christians expect that we Indians should receive and accept
the doctrinal definitions of particular churches, viz. *American* (or
British origin) Methodist, *American* Free Methodist, *American*
Baptist, *American* Free Will Baptist, *German* Lutheran, *British*
Anglican, *Greek* Orthodox, *Syrian* Jacobite, *Roman* Catholic,
etc.; only then, will we be accepted as a sincere and orthodox

Indian Christian!?! This is why Christianity is often criticized as "churchianity." In India, one can hardly find an Indian church because here we have *Greek* philosophy, *Roman* administration, *Jewish* customs and rituals (including the dress of the pastor), German theology, *European* culture and NOTHING INDIAN.

Without Indian Christian theology, no deep growth in discipleship in Christ can be expected. This seems now to be granted in theory by almost everyone, but actual progress is hardly evident. To form Indian Christian theology, we must use terms from the Indian scriptures and philosophical systems, which itself is a Himalayan task before us. With rejecting Indian terms at random as "pagan nonsense" or from the devil, such a task cannot even be begun.

Yet, developing Indian theology is a deeper and more complex matter than just adopting new terminology. It is perhaps the Western imprint on Christianity that makes it possible for us to easily understand rational and linguistic aspects of contextualization; and ceremonial or ritual changes are understandable because they can be seen. But there are subtle nuances that defy definition, especially by a layman like me. There is an ethos or feel, a way of looking and perceiving, that goes far beyond external changes of culture or terminology. Perhaps these words from Carl Keller will help explain what I am groping to say:

> It may be that the Vedanta provides a better method for the study of the message of Christ than our methods of thinking derived from Greece and the Renaissance. It may be that the Indian way of thinking is much nearer to the Bible's thinking than ours, and therefore, much better qualified to probe the ultimate depths of the Bible. Should that be so, then it might become evident that a theological method of research enriched and whetted by the Vedanta might help not only the Indian church but also Christianity everywhere.[18]

However, using all the terms and categories of Hindu philosophy is equally dangerous. While forming any theology using native words and scriptures, we cannot avoid the tension between going too far and not going far enough. (See Appendix B on OM for an example.) David Hesselgrave, after explaining the two extremes of going too far and not going far enough in bridge building, concludes that "biblical bridge building reveals a profound knowledge of human nature, culture, and religion on the one hand, and a significant effort to adapt to them on the other." He refers to contextualization as "apostolic accommodation":

> Any accommodation that is made to the cultures and religions of the world must be consonant with that [Great] Commission–its requirements, its message, its means, and its ends. That is why, in biblical bridge building, communication always centered on what God had said in His Word; the call was always to conversion; the demands were never adjusted to human preferences; and dialogue often entailed disputation....two elements that are absolutely essential to authentic contextualization efforts: the supra cultural nature of the biblical gospel and the cultural requirements of meaningful communication. Of course, the biblical gospel is not acultural. It was given to and through prophets and apostles–men who received and reported the divine message in linguistic and cultural frames of reference. But the sovereign God ordered the cultural circumstances, the prophetic and apostolic personnel, and the linguistic forms in such a way that in both the revelational and inscripturation processes it was his message that was transmitted. The biblical message, therefore, is unique. The impingements of circumscribed cultures, imperfect authors, and human language are transcended in such a way as to provide a perfect gospel.[19]

At present, there can be no doubt that our primary concern must be that we have not gone nearly far enough in contextualizing our theology. This is not by any means a new problem, however, as this was already being recognized nearly a century ago. Already in 1908, realizing the need of an Indian Christian theology, S. K. Datta wrote:

> The Indian Church has failed on the whole to produce a distinctive theology capable of reaching the minds and hearts of the people....Indian Christianity is as yet a Western product in the process of being grafted on to India....New interpretations of Christian doctrine will scarcely be possible till the intellectual level of the Indian Church is raised.[20]

C.F. Andrews wrote in a tone of regret:

> Few Indian Christian thinkers have yet been able to apply the terms of Hindu philosophy to the expression of Christian doctrine in the way that Tertullian, Athanasius and Basil used the terminology of philosophic thought current in the later Roman Empire.[21]

Nevertheless, nearly a century later, the theological colleges in India are still producing Westernized theologians who can never properly fit into their home situation. M. M. Thomas wrote of Andrews that "…he was very critical of the curriculum of the Indian theological colleges which *destroyed indigenous original Christian thought.*"[22] Nothing seems to have changed.

Considering the need and relevance, one has to wonder about the contribution of the present theological colleges and institutes towards evangelism in India. We have never heard or come across one single seminary where systematic teaching on Hindu scriptures is part of the curriculum. Though comparative religion is taught as one subject (in which Hinduism will also be a part), no special course is offered exclusively on Hinduism with a particular focus on the Hindu scriptures. As several voices have been raised in the past days which were deliberately neglected, there is no point of wasting more time and space on it here also, except raising again the question of R.C. Das :

> When these days, one hears of appeal for lakhs [hundreds of thousands] of rupees and dollars for these theological colleges, one shudders to think of the future of the Indian church. Will the West continue to give money on this lavish scale till Doom's Day and will it produce an Indian church?[23]

The wonder in it is that while Indian theologians are busy going to Western theological seminaries to obtain advanced degrees and doctorates in Western theology in order to get recognition in Indian churches, no genuine encouragement is available among Indian Christians to study and form Indian Christian theology. We continue bound to Western concepts and tools. A good example is the 100 Bible Lessons. While a lot of Indian Christians as well as publishers are busy in translating Western theological books (with a few by Indians, though written in Western style and pattern) only Western scholars are making any contribution to help us to form Indian Christian theology, like that of Prof. Klaus K. Klostermaier's *Indian Theology In Dialogue* (CLS, Madras, 1986).

The apostles clearly were not afraid to use existing pagan words to communicate their message, even when those terms had some false meanings associated with them. S. N. Wald makes this point strongly and clearly:

> It is remarkable that the revealed religion of the Old Testament, when it was presented to a wider circle in the Greek language through the translation of the LXX, did not take over specific Hebrew words to express

the revelation made in that language. The translators found in the Koine ready—made forms to express the message of God. Only a few Hebrew words were taken over, such as Sabaoth, Amen, Alleluja and a few others, which words, however, do not express strictly religious ideas. The same development continued in the New Testament. The writers of the New Testament take the common religious terms of their time, the terms of a language which was polytheistic in its background, and with this material they build up the Christian terminology. They took words from Greek philosophy, from pagan rites and pagan mysteries to express Christian concepts. Especially the terminology of the mysteries was largely transported into Christian use. In this way, words like *theos, kyrios, logos, soter, eulogia, mysterion, charis, prophetia, baptismos, episcopos, diaconos,* were taken to express specific Christian ideas.[24]

Robin Boyd, in his standard work on Indian theology, makes the same point, but traces it in the history of Christian theology:

Western theology has never been able to dissociate itself from philosophy, from the time of the Platonism of Justin Martyr onwards. Plato lies behind Augustine, Aristotle behind Aquinas and even Calvin; right down to the days of idealism, existentialism and logical positivism, no theologian, not even those like Barth who have tried to break free from philosophy, has succeeded in dissociating himself from the philosophical presuppositions of certain schools. In the West, the philosophy with which theology has been associated has not necessarily been Christian philosophy; theologians have felt the need, in their systematic statements, of using the language and the thought—patterns of a Plato, an Aristotle, a Kant, a Hegel, a Gogarten, a Buber, a Wittgenstein....May it not be possible for Indian theologians, while remaining faithful to the biblical "deposit," to work out their apologetic and their systematic theological statements in the terminology of certain schools of Hindu thought?...

As we reflect on the process by which Christianity in the early centuries became acclimatized in the Greek world, and by which it made use of certain categories of Greek thought, we are struck by the double fact of its acceptance of "secularized" Greek philosophy and philosophical terminology, and its complete rejection of Greek religion and mythology....The medieval monks who concealed their copies of Virgil in the thatch of their cells, and read them surreptitiously when religious authority was not looking, were not reverting to Graeco—Roman paganism, but were simply seeking an artistic, cultural outlet and stimulus of which their monastic life deprived them.[25] The old gods died, but their ghosts passed into the literary and cultural heritage of Europe, and it was the Church, strangely enough, which preserved them. Greek religion was isolated from philosophy, secularized, preserved, and eventually became incorporated, at the renaissance, into modern European culture. Christian poets, philosophers, painters and even theologians have not hesitated to use "encapsulated" Greek religion and mythology in their works. From Milton to T. S. Eliot,

and even to theologians like Reinhold Niebuhr, the types and stories of
Greek religious mythology have provided a background and illustration for
Christian exposition. Christian culture has seldom banished the Muses and
the Graces, and the stuff of Greek tragedy has at times served to expound
and to deepen our understanding of the work of Christ.[26]

Starting with the unknown Jewish translators of the Old Testament into Greek (the Septuagint, often abbreviated as LXX),
through Paul and John and all through the centuries to today, if
European Christians had the right to use Greek philosophy and
terminology and even Greek religious and mythological references in their works, then why should we Indians not be allowed
to use Indian terms and philosophy to communicate the gospel
to our own people? Above all, the "Western theological traditions have developed according to Greek, rather than Hebrew
thought," all the "pillars of God's truth" in the Western denominations, "and the rationales for their existence is built on the
brittle logic of Greeks [long dead]." [27] Therefore, we have every
right to form our own Indian theology, which comes close to the
"Hebrew way of thinking." [28]

As one untrained in theology, perhaps I have no right to even
talk about it. Numerous theologians, both national and foreign,
are talking and writing a lot about Indian theology, but little
seems to come of it. The subject cannot be closed, however,
without clearly agreeing with the many warnings about the danger of going too far in accommodating to contextual thought
forms. To quote from Hesselgrave again,

It is ironic that the gospel itself can be lost in the effort to accommodate
it to other cultures and religions. But precisely that sometimes happened
in the early centuries, and precisely that is happening today. The risk of
going too far is very real.[29]

As we saw, the church fathers freely used Greek philosophical terms to form their theology. But, as Robin Boyd points out,
Greek philosophy was "often almost entirely secular," whereas
"Hindu philosophy and religion are more closely interwoven…
and Sankara and Ramanuja are regarded as great religious figures
as much as philosophers." [30] Therefore, how far to go and where

to draw lines is not a simple question to be answered by one person or group. A joint venture by many is essential in this task.

Sadly, it is not difficult to find examples of inappropriate and confusing writing presented under the name of developing Indian theology. A recent striking example is the attempt of K. P. Aleaz to present Christian thought through *Advaita* Vedanta. Everyone would welcome a clear answer to the question of "who is Jesus?" through the "hermeneutical context of India." [31] But when the attempt to do so involves the undermining of the basic tenants of the gospel and the faith and experience of the early Christ *bhaktas*, it can only confuse both Christians and Hindus. The confusion, which Aleaz creates, reaches its climax when he says:

> Our Jesulogy basically agrees with the contention of the Neo—Vedantins that unfortunately the universal message of Jesus which comprises the ideas of the indwelling divinity, of divine grace, universal ethics, and spiritual realization was distorted by the Christian Church through fettering it in cast—iron dogmas of innate vileness of human nature, the "scapegoat" and the "atonement," physical resurrection and the second advent, earthly kingdom and imminence of the Day of judgment which are purely sectarian in their scope. Human sacrifice was a Jewish idea and to fit the gentle and loving Jesus into Jewish beliefs, the idea of human sacrifice in the form of atonement or as a human scapegoat, by Christianity, was really unfortunate. [32]

In order to "make sense to Indians" Aleaz has re—crucified Jesus on the cross of Sankara's *Advaita*. One cannot resist concluding that "Christianity is really unfortunate" to have these kinds of theologians.

Theologians should always remember that their theology must be "of the faith, for the faith and by the faith" of people and not their own private intellectual entertainment, as is well defined by Francis Clooney:

> Theology, to characterize it in a non—technical fashion, is distinct from the study of religion (with which it overlaps in many of its procedures) because theology is an inquiry carried on by believers who allow their belief to remain an explicit and influential factor in their research, analysis and writing. Believing theologians are (usually) members of believing communities, and have those communities as their primary audiences, whether or not the bulk of their writing is addressed to them. With their communities, they believe in some transcendent (perhaps supernatural) reality, the possibility of and (usually fact of) a normative revelation, and in the need to

make practical decisions and life choices, which have a bearing on salvation. Theologians do their work with an awareness of and concern for
these beliefs, and with a desire to defend and preserve them, even if at
one or another moment, they may have to question, recontextualize and
finally reformulate them in modes of discourse quite different from those
already familiar to the community.[33]

Every Hindu Christ *bhakta* lives with an open tension in his
commitment to Jesus based on biblical instruction on the one
hand and the struggle to properly maintain his Indian identity, not just for the sake of personal psychological survival but
because of his birthright. Therefore, he always welcomes new efforts of the theologians to help him both to understand his faith
in Christ as well as to share it with other members of his community with the help of native forms. But being a layman, he
needs a strong foundation to keep his faith alive amidst various
struggles for survival as a Christ *bhakta* in his own community.
Nothing but the Bible can provide such a foundation, however
poor his hermeneutical theories applied to the Bible may be.
When that very biblical foundation begins to be shaken because
of the subversion of the scriptures in the name of doctrine and
hermeneutics, then he is left with no option but to ignore the
theologians in order to keep his faith alive. Because all the alterations in a new house must be made within the limits of the foundation and not outside of it, any building constructed outside
of the foundation, however beautiful it may look, will never be
safe. Moreover, in the case of faith in Christ, if the word of God,
which is "given" in the apostolic tradition, is challenged in the
name of the "importance to the hermeneutical context" (as by
Aleaz), then he would rather give up all alterations to the building and choose to live in a simple hut with a strong foundation.

A complicating factor in the development of Indian theology
is the fact that within Hindu philosophical traditions a single
term can have vastly varying meanings in the various Hindu
systems of thought. While borrowing Indian terms, we cannot ignore either the particular (scriptural and philosophical)
or popular (as understood and lived in daily reality) contexts of
those terms. It is indeed commendable that in Christian un-

derstanding of the Scriptures, the context is recognized to be of central importance. While interpreting any Bible verse, we have to see textual, historical and theological contexts. That some Christians ignore the contexts of Hindu scriptures and ignore the Hindu hermeneutical traditions must be condemned. The following section addresses this particular problem.

It must be granted that contexts do not hold the same weight when Hindu scriptures are interpreted by Hindus. Israel Selvanayagam points this out in saying that "When Hindu thinkers use RV [Rig Veda] 1.164.46 they are never concerned about its context." [34] For a Hindu, truth is important not events; the principle is important not the person who shared it; why something is said outweighs any question of when it was said. This view helps them to claim a universal nature for their Scriptures, as their teachings are applicable to all the people all the time. Of course in theory, they keep the principle that while any teaching of the *smriti* [later "remembered" scriptures] contradicts with the sruti [earlier "heard" scriptures], the former must be rejected. But in practice, this principle is not strictly enforced because all the *smritis* in a very real sense are also Vedas for them. (It must also be recognized that true scholars like P. V. Kane and others always emphasized and interpreted the Hindu Scriptures according to their contexts.)

Hence, keeping all the textual and contextual problems before us in forming Indian Christian theology, we face a lot of problems. For example, desiring to use the emotionally appealing word Advaita, some use it to indicate monism (One alone exists), but others to indicate non–dualism (there are two but they are not really two).[35] Either of these sounds like the commonly criticized supposedly Hindu doctrine of pantheism, yet one can find something quite near this in certain biblical passages ("For in him we live and move and have our being," Acts 17: 28; "One God and Father of all, who is over all and through all and in all," Eph.4:6). In taking account of all potential pitfalls plus our own obvious limitations as well as the complex dynamics of linguistic development, we must never lose sight of the fact that local people must be allowed to form their own theology to help in their existential needs. After all, theology is a tool to give outer expression in doctrinal statements to the inner experience with the truth. And as "experience" cannot be fully, adequately expressed in any way, it should be transmitted through life not transferred through words. The words of George Lindbeck make this point very clear:

> Just as grammar by itself affirms nothing either true or false regarding the world in which language is used, but only about language, so theology and doctrine, to the extent that they are second—order activities, assert nothing either true or false about God and his relation to creatures, but only speak about such assertions. These assertions, in turn, cannot be made except when speaking religiously, i.e., when seeking to align oneself and others performatively with what one takes to be most important in the universe by worshipping, promising, obeying, exhorting, preaching.[36]

Understanding this, it remains to be pointed out that in attempts to form a theology that is relevant to our land, we need not always do it with reference to the Hindu religious terms and that too with a reference to the so called "Brahminical" system. Jesus came to redeem people from every form of slavery (though sin is the basis for all of them). Hence the call for a "social" theology and a "liberation" (or "Dalit") theology with a special reference to our Indian context should not be neglected in the name of Indian theology. Whether biblical theology in India is for Dalits or Vedantins or OBCs [Other Backward Castes], yet each group has its own Indian bowl to receive it. Are we willing to give the Living Water in their own bowl, or will we insist on serving it only in Western cups?

E. IN IGNORING OR MISUSING HINDU SCIPTURES

God's revelation is everywhere. Though His final revelation, according to our conviction, was in Christ and the Bible, yet we can find traces of His revelation in other scriptures also to some extent. In India particularly, the longing for God and the efforts made to reach Him were endless. All these longings and efforts came to expression in the form of beautiful scriptures, which are unique in the whole world.

Without reading these scriptures, we cannot understand the minds of Hindus. Even a secularized Hindu cannot avoid the influence of his scriptures (varying texts in varying communities) as he was born and brought up in an environment in which the scriptures play a vital role. From cradle to grave, his life is mingled with his scriptures. As God can prepare a person to receive His grace only in the background in which he was born and brought up, the Indian scriptures play a vital role in preparing a person to receive the gospel. Therefore, without proper study of their scriptures, we cannot do effective ministry among them.

Nobody can minimize the contribution of numerous missionaries in this area, for which we Indians are very much thankful. Many Western missionaries and Indologists were scholars, and some invested their whole life in the task of understanding and explaining Hinduism. With rare exceptions, most of them remained loyal to their work and never misused the Hindu scriptures for their vested interests, although their presuppositions surely subtly influenced their works. Their basic attitude can be seen in these words of W. J. Wilkins in his preface to a study on Hindu mythology:

> It has been my endeavor to give a fair and impartial account of these deities, as far as possible in the words of the sacred books; such an account as I should expect an honest–minded Hindu to give of God from a careful study of the Bible. I have honestly striven to keep free from prejudice and theological bias; and, wishing to let the sacred books speak for themselves, have refrained from commenting on the passages quoted, excepting where some explanation seemed necessary. I have not selected those texts which describe the darker side only of the Hindu gods, nor have such been altogether suppressed....Of what was fit for publication I have taken a proportionate amount, that this, together with what is worthy of commendation, may give a faithful picture. To magnify either the good or the evil is the work of the advocate — a work I, in this book, distinctly disclaim. An honest effort has been made to give a reliable account of the things commonly believed by millions of our Hindu fellow–subjects.[37]

Sadly, few such scholars can be found any more among devout Christians. From the beginning of this century, attempts were made, often by these fine missionary scholars, to find evidences in the Indian scriptures for a fulfillment theology, i.e. that Jesus Christ somehow fulfills what is true and good in

Hinduism and its scriptures. Even before J. N. Farquhar, the
best–known fulfillment thinker, scholars like K. M. Banerjea (in
his book The Arian Witness) searched Indian scriptures to find
evidences for their fulfillment theory. But nowadays, there have
come several "fulfillmentalists" who, without any sincere work
on their part but simply borrowing others' ideas, misuse and
misinterpret Indian scriptures for their own purposes.

As we rightly expect others to be honest with our scriptures,
at the same time, we too must be honest towards their scriptures. Either rejecting them as "pagan nonsense" or twisting
and turning them to point to our own particular doctrines is
wrong in every way. Above all, the lay people in every religion
do not know their own scriptures properly and thoroughly. This
applies to all – Hindus, Muslims and Christians. Thus, in our
approach to them, either to present the gospel or to defend our
doctrines, we should not cheat them by misquoting or half–
quoting from their scriptures.

> Sadly, numerous examples are available of Christian misuse of Hindu
> scripture. For a striking example, note the claim by Joseph Padinjarekara
> that "the Vedas and the Upanishads talk about the Resurrection, not
> Reincarnation" :
>
> In a strict sense, we can't find a single verse in the Vedas to support the
> theory of re–incarnation. However, many verses in the Upanishads are
> wrongly interpreted to prove this theory. But if we start our studies from
> the clear passages about immortality in Vedic literature, we can easily see
> that the Vedas support the idea of the resurrection of the body.
>
> The main theme of the Kathopanishad is a search for life after death.
> It clearly states who will "escape from the mouth of death" ("...mrtu-
> mukhaatpramucyate") [Katha Upanishad 3:15].
>
> The author of the Upanishad came to the conclusion that after death,
> there is immortality, not reincarnation. This state of immortality is called
> Mukti.[38]

Anyone with even a basic knowledge of the Upanishads
will immediately see how terribly twisted this teaching is. It is
perhaps worth noting that Padinjarekara's book was published
in Canada and (thankfully) has never appeared widely in India.
His point is true that the Vedas proper (the *Samhitas* or hymn
portion of the Vedas) do not teach reincarnation. But the Upa-

nishads (the last section of the Vedic corpus) most certainly do, and do so with abundant clarity in the same Upanishad (and same chapter within that Upanishad) as Padinjarekara quoted in his false teaching! Katha Upanishad 3:17 says:

> He, however, who has not understanding,
> Who is unmindful and ever impure,
> Reaches not the goal,
> But goes on to reincarnation (samsara).[39]

One might wish that such completely erroneous teaching was only published to mislead gullible Americans, but there are plenty of similar examples of the twisting of Indian scripture easily available in India. Acharya Daya Prakash (Rev. D. P. Titus), in his writings, is more restrained and sensible than Padinjarekara but still goes far beyond what can be considered as acceptable interpretations of Hindu scripture.[40] For example, Titus suggests that "in spiritual application, Christ is the true Soma (Vine, creeper) (Jn.15:1) whose life was crushed upon the Cross." This is considered to be like the Soma of the Veda which "was plucked and crushed by fingers and pounded in a vessel, Rig Veda 9.1.2; 9.67.3."[41]

Further false fulfillments and abuses of Hindu scripture could be listed at great length. Various tracts go around, often written by Hindu converts whom claim to be Sanskrit scholars, which list various strikingly Christian comments from Hindu scriptures. But often, the supposed references are not even mentioned for one to try to check them. Other times, clearly false translations or references are given.[42] A favorite claim is that Jesus Christ is the *Prajapati* sacrifice prefigured in the Rig Veda. This theory has been analyzed and shown to involve a serious distortion of the Hindu scriptures by Sri H. L. Richard.[43]

Similarly, several tracts are coming out quoting the sayings of great Indian personalities like Swami Vivekananda but without sharing their complete view about Jesus. For example, one leaflet entitled "Vivekanandar kanda Yesu" (Jesus accepted by Vivekananda) in which all of Vivekananda's commendations about Jesus are quoted. However, the truth is that Vivekananda's Jesus is of his own creation and is not the Jesus of the Bible. One should be very careful while quoting the words of such people to recommend other Indians to follow Christ.

Such distortions of Hindu scriptures by some, does not mean that we should not use Indian Scriptures in a proper way in our ministry. There are plenty of songs and *slokas* which are helpful to use in our satsanghs, especially to point out the reality of man's sin, the danger of postponing the question of salvation to some other births based on the belief in rebirth, God's grace in redeeming the sinner, etc. We must use such passages from Hindu Scriptures in order to help a Hindu to understand biblical doctrines properly. The Bible, itself, clearly affirms this practice as it shows Paul in Athens (Acts 17) teaching in this way.

We can prepare a person to receive the gospel only through the background in which he was born and brought up. Similarly, to prepare him to receive Jesus, the Hindu scriptures can play a vital role, even as Robin Boyd showed Greek mythology could do ("Christian culture has seldom banished the Muses and the Graces, and the stuff of Greek tragedy has at times served to expound and to deepen our understanding of the work of Christ." [44])

We cannot approach a Muslim with the Gita or a Hindu with the Koran. At the same time, rejecting both Gita and Koran will deprive the Hindu and the Muslim of important bridges to understanding the gospel clearly, so we must use them. At the same time, we should not misuse them willy–nilly to accomplish our purposes. Be honest with the scriptures of every religion.

If Jesus Christ fulfilled certain aspects of a myth about god or there is a Hindu scripture with which we agree, then what about those aspects of the same god or other parts of that scripture which do not agree with us? If Jesus Christ gives content to "the Hindu name for Siva, the kind one..." [45] (as a prayer offered in church suggested) then what about Rudra ("the Terror") [46] another name of the same Siva? Simply for our convenience sake, we cannot separate one attribute of a Hindu god from its overall context (as well as from the understanding of the people who worship him), and use it for our end. This is "Christian arrogancy," to use the words of Dr. Paul Sudhakar.

The fulfillment theories inevitably twist Hindu scriptures, and interestingly, base their philosophy on a misinterpretation of the Bible. The word "fulfill" that Jesus used in the Sermon on the Mount (Mt. 5:17) does not support the concept that He fulfills all religions and scriptures. A proper understanding of Jesus' words as expounded by Martyn Lloyd–Jones makes this clear:

> ...the term "fulfill." There has been a great deal of confusion with regard to its meaning, so we must point out at once that it does not mean to complete, to finish; it does not mean to add to something that has already been begun. This popular interpretation is an entire misunderstanding of the word. It has been said that the Old Testament began a certain teaching and that it carried on so far and up to a point. Then our Lord came and carried it a stage further, rounding it off and fulfilling it, as it were. That is not the true interpretation. The real meaning of the word "fulfill" is to carry out, to fulfill in the sense of giving full obedience to it, literally carrying out everything that has been said and stated in the law and in the prophets. [47]

Can we say that Jesus literally gave full obedience and carried out everything that has been said and stated in the Hindu scriptures in His life and death? Forming any theology based on words isolated from their context will mislead us all. Some Hindus do a good job of similarly distorting the teachings of the Bible, and the study of these things causes one to appreciate the efforts to develop honest and intelligent dialogue between Hindus and Christians. [48] Don't cheat the lay people anywhere.

To present the gospel effectively to Hindus, a proper knowledge about Hinduism, particularly with reference to their scriptures, is essential. Moreover, not mere academic knowledge, but a practical knowledge about the other's scripture is necessary. This, one could obtain only through the process of involvement in interfaith dialogue. Particularly in our effort to use the Hindu Scriptures for our evangelical endeavors, learning from the Hindus about their Scriptures is essential to avoid misuse of them. And for this, dialogue is an absolute necessity.

Having spoken of my appreciation for sincere dialogue, I must go on to comment further on this phenomenon, which has become either a powerful movement or perhaps is just a massive intellectual fad. Raimundo Panikkar divides the whole of church history into five broad periods marked by 1) witness, 2) conversion, 3) crusade, 4) mission, and 5) dialogue.[49] Though the concept of dialogue as a science has become popular after Christendom faced the challenges of other faiths in its missionary endeavor, yet we can even trace it from the New Testament time in the ministry of Paul.

In our effort to share the gospel with our own people in India, whether we like it or not, dialogue is the only method which will open the hearts and minds of our people to Jesus. However, the word dialogue has become anathema among many Christians, particularly in evangelical circles. Still, every Yesu *bhakta* in Hindu community would understand that in his every day life, he is involved in a *living dialogue* with his own people. Those Christians who are involved in "extraction evangelism" (pulling out a single follower of Jesus from his family and community in the name of safeguarding his faith) and *kabaddi* evangelism cannot understand the need for such dialogue because they are coming from a "compound Christianity" and create again the same in all their evangelistic endeavors. Hence, they are standing outside the world of a dialogue approach in sharing their faith.

However, the dialogue movement can hardly be considered to have arrived at anything resembling success. Though there are serious dialogists, most of them have failed due to several limitations on their part. For one thing, hardly any Indian Protestant Christians have cared at all about dialogue. Israel Selvanayagam laments this and gives an insightful explanation for it:

> The observable fear of Protestant Christians on dialogue is twofold. Some feel threatened that dialogue with Hindus would amount to total absorption of the faith of the little flock of Christians into the vastly broad framework of Hinduism. Others see no point of having dialogue with a religion from which they or their parents or foreparents were converted. It seems to be a tedious task to remove the phobia and muster the courage for dialogue.[50]

Though encouraging efforts were initiated in the Roman Catholic church following the directives of the Vatican II

(1962–65), because of their "church oriented approach" they are rather elitist and not much contribution comes from lay people, although "almost every diocese has a Commission on Dialogue for encouraging Christians to have fruitful encounter with their Hindu neighbors." [51]

Whenever some church people talk about dialogue, the immediate picture that comes to mind is of a gathering of marginalized intellectuals who are not going to take others' contributions seriously "except for enjoying a holiday at the expense of the mission" as admitted by some astute dialogists themselves.[52]

Though the dialogue approach is good for learning Hinduism from the practical as well as personal views of Hindus, yet most of the time in organized inter–religious dialogues there is too much intellectual gamesmanship. Though they all will claim to listen to others' views with an open heart and mind, yet both the parties know that others are not going to buy their views at any time. This does not mean that all inter–religious interactions are a mere waste of time. What I want to say is that dialogue on an intellectual level in seminaries and conferences is not the best way to understand Hinduism or bring about true understanding of the gospel. The main problem (or rather stumbling block) to understand another's faith through dialogical religiosity is that most of the approach is theoretical or merely academic.

Comparing and contrasting with the apostle Paul is instructive. He engaged in dialogue constantly. Note that he never recruited more full time workers or dialogue partners from the Jerusalem church to share their faith among the non–Jews. Likewise, there is no indication that he encouraged the conservative Jews with whom he always had confrontations (like that with our Indian Christians whom Christ *bhaktas* now confront) to get involved in dialogue with their Gentile neighbors. Rather, he made disciples among the non–Jews and allowed them to live as they were, as non–Jews, to have a Living Dialogue with their own people, because surely they had a better understanding of their own society, community, culture and religion than any Jewish outsiders could. Thankfully, he never transplanted the non–Jews from their environment and made them "Christians." This is how the early church grew among the non–Jews. Both early church history and the development of early Christian doctrines are witnesses of this.

The dialogue movement contains many needed antidotes for problems, like Christians and Hindus abusing each other's scriptures and misunderstanding each other's true doctrines and feelings. Nevertheless, it is difficult to imagine how it can ever move beyond an elitist academic exercise when neither lay Christians nor lay or "clerical" Hindus show any interest in it. Paul's model of direct involvement across communal boundaries in incarnational witness must be deemed far superior to the bridge building efforts of the dialogue movement.

F. IN RELATION TO HINDU RELGIOUS PRACTICES

Perhaps the most urgent steps that must be taken by Christians to prepare for outreach to neighbors of other faiths is the removal of Pharisaism from within the church. While Hindu friends are criticized for their blind faiths imposed on them by their tradition, there remain an abundance of so called "Christian" traditions with similar blind faith. Particularly in the area of *samskaras* (ceremonies) related to birth, marriage and death, each society has its own tradition to follow.

The Bible is actually quite silent in this area of *samskaras*. What we have as dedication of children, confirmation for the full–fledged membership in the church, the so–called "Christian" style marriage (which is actually a Western or secular marriage) and "Christian" burial, are some of the blind traditions that we are still keeping. We could add several more things to this list. Instead of following Western traditions, however valuable they may be, we must learn to follow our own social and cultural traditions, which are flexible enough to be adapted for conveying biblical meanings. For example, we should not bury a twice born convert (someone from one of the upper three castes), nor create separate graveyards for them. Instead, burn the body (a traditional Hindu funeral is cremation). Many

"Christian" funerals are devoid of hope, and it is not burial which points to the hope of resurrection so much as the "peace of God that transcends all understanding" (Phil. 4:7) among those witnessing the last rites.[53] Similarly, arrange Indian style marriage ceremonies in the churches (or, better still, outside the church buildings). This will encourage people to follow Christ without breaking away from their society.

This perspective is often challenged by reference to the words of Jesus that He came "to set a man against his father, etc..."(Matt. 10:32–39). We are called out people, separated unto God; therefore, the world will reject us and even persecute us, etc. Such comments are the common points against keeping cultural and social identity with the people, but these verses and points are all quoted out of context. If I am persecuted for my faith in Christ and for my changed life because of Christ, as I am no more partaking with others in their sins or worldly life, then indeed, we must rejoice and thank God (I Pet. 3:13–17; 4: 3–4, 14–16) as our Lord's words are being fulfilled (Matt. 5: 10–12) in our lives. However, if we are rejected, opposed, perse- cuted and misunderstood because of not remaining loyal to our own culture, society and nation, by not observing even those things of our society which are biblical or about which the Bible is silent, then are we to rejoice or regret?

The Red Dot

Probably the most heated issue for debate in the whole area of Hindu cultural/religious practices relates to the *pottu* or *bindi,* the red dot worn on the forehead by most Indian women. Now in south India, following a custom that could only be called "Hindu," even Christian ladies keep flowers in their hair. Once they become widows they automatically lose their right to do so. Similarly, only south Indian women keep flowers in their hair and most north Indian women do not (particularly in Hindi speaking areas). In the north, only prostitutes decorate their hair with flowers. These things show that cultural prac- tices differ across regions and are not defined solely according to religious affiliations. They differ from place to place and from person to person.

Now every objective observer can see that keeping the *pottu* (red dot) is purely cultural for a woman, while not being so for a man. When a lady becomes a widow, she loses her right to keep the bindi and sindur (red powder above the forehead where the hair is parted), but she can keep *bhuti* or *vibhuti* (ash) on her forehead, as this is indeed a "religious" symbol. This proves that the former two are related to the cultural aspect. Another clear example is that the Vaishnavite ladies (followers of Vishnu) may keep both *srichurnam* (or *namam,* vertical lines on the forehead) along with *sindur* and *bindi,* but when they become widows, they may still keep the *namam* but not the others. Thus, these are marks of marital status, not religious devotion.

Most Indian Christians are born and brought up in "Christian colonies" and have a strong aversion towards the red dot (*pottu/bindi*) right from childhood. One brother even said to me, "from childhood we received the teaching regularly that the Hindus are worshipping the devil. So anything related to their culture and social life, including religion, creates a deep aversion within us." [54] Such deep aversion prevents people from changing their prejudices against Hindu protocol. Any amount of argument and proof will not convince them that keeping *sindur* (red powder) and *pottu* (*bindi*) has nothing to do with their religious practices, but rather only the cultural aspect of life.[55] Consequentially, without removing these kinds of prejudices, if we dare to teach, we will, in fact, close the other members of the same society against following Christ as they will see everything in this "new religion" as a threat to their cultural and social identity.

One more tragedy is that these prejudices seem to be based on hearsay alone. All the preconceived objections against Hindu cultural matters are based on second and third hand information that has been heard from others. The objection to a *pottu* (*bindi*) is based on the idea that there is a religious connection behind it. The *bindi* is the blood of Kali or the third eye of Siva, etc. But if asked to prove this by giving a reference from the

Hindu scriptures or mythology, the only response is "we don't
know. We only heard this from others, even from the new converts." Some few, on the other hand, quote Ezek. 9:3–6 and say,
"at baptism, as the sign of the cross is placed on our forehead,
we should not keep *pottu.*" What kind of Christian superstition
is this? Does the Bible say that at the time of baptism the cross
sign must be placed on our forehead? What right do you have
to criticize the Hindus while holding such kinds of superstition
and blind faith yourself!

It is also worth noting that the tali or *mangalyam* (wedding
chain) worn as a symbol of marriage, even by Christian women,
has far stronger religious associations than the *pottu* does.
Nowadays, it is common practice, during the month of March
in a Tamil Brahmin's house, that all the women (except widows)
observe *karadayan nonbu.* That day they fast and in the evening
perform *puja* [worship] even for their *tali* (*mangalyam*). The religious sanction for this comes from the mythology of *Satyavan–
Savitri.* Even at the time of marriage some sort of ceremony is
performed with the tali. If the Christians find comfort and even
have sentimental attachment with such a *mangalyam* and prefer
to keep it, why do they entertain such an aversion towards the
pottu, which has only cultural significance? If Christian women
feel happy with a *tali,* will it not be an injustice if they ask new
converts to remove the *pottu?* If they find it uncomfortable
to keep the *pottu,* we understand their psychological problem
which so far shaped such aversion towards it. Nevertheless, they
must have sympathetic understanding towards the psychology of
a new believer for whom removing the *pottu* is difficult. Therefore, they should not compel the removal of the *pottu,* but rather
should encourage them to keep it.

The following incident, which is recorded in the Oct. 1996
edition of the magazine *Insight,* demonstrates the importance
of these seemingly minor issues, particularly for missionaries
who are working in north India. A missionary couple, working among Hindus, had the joy of expecting a child. When the
wife went for her medical checkup, the local lady doctor asked

if they would like to abort the baby. Not understanding why
the doctor was asking such a question, they merely said no and
had the baby. The same incident was repeated for all the three
children they had.

Confused by the repeated question of the doctor about
abortion, they finally enquired and were shocked at what they
learned. There was no social evil involved, just miscommunication. As the missionary's wife did not wear *sindur, bindi,
bangles* or *mangalyam,* the signs of a married woman in India,
the doctor thought that they were living together without being married. Thus, in order to help them to solve the problem
of having a child outside marriage, she offered to help them
procure an abortion. The same was the impression of the local
people among whom they served as witnesses for Christ. The local people thought that Christianity even allowed such an illicit
and illegal relationship outside of marriage. Obviously, there was
little true communication of the gospel in such an atmosphere.
Hence, following the Pauline concept of "becoming all things
to all men"(1 Cor. 9:22), the missionaries should not only stop
asking new converts to remove the signs of marriage, but they
themselves should put them on. (For further thoughts on the red
dot, see Sri P. Chenchiah's striking comments in Appendix A.)

Now some Christians, after a lot of struggle, finally say (not
agree) that an orthodox Hindu woman convert can be allowed
to keep the *pottu* (*bindi*) if her unconverted Hindu husband in-
sists, but as days go, if that husband does not insist on the *pottu*,
she can remove it. Such issues, say these Christians who won't
allow the woman to keep the *pottu*, are between the husband and
wife to decide and are not for the pastor or the church. However, my question is, "What is there to even decide?" Any such
decision is nothing but brainwashing or putting indirect pressure
on the woman by the congregation. No one would ever think
of removing the *pottu* except for Christian pressure. If anyone
acts on the concession mentioned here and keeps the *pottu*, if a
small problem or tragedy comes in the life of such a new believer,
it will invariably be imputed to not obeying God by removing

the *pottu*. (If such tragedy or problems come in the lives of those who removed the *pottu*, some other excuses will be given.) Pity the new believer who takes such words as final authority in her spiritual life and goes against her husband/family decision and creates unnecessary problems for herself and her family.

There is another very serious problem in this "concession of the *pottu*" position held by many Christians. It is taught that this concession given to a woman to wear the *pottu* should only be temporary. Once a strong "Christian community" comes up which can provide an alternate "Christian culture," then the *pottu* and thali should go! (No *pottu*, no thali etc. are considered as Christian culture – in that case, all our Hindu widows are already Christians or following some Christian culture.) But since no Christian culture exists, why should a new alternate cultural style develop in the name of "Christian community?" If such a distinct Christian community rises in one locality and removes certain cultural practices (like the *pottu* and thali) of Hindus, how are their relatives living in another area going to respond to such changes? Hindu society is not only restricted to local communities, but there are close contacts with extended families living in different places. Such unnecessary, unbiblical changes just to please or accommodate the feelings of the fifth generation Christians will only hinder the furtherance of the gospel. So for the sake of the gospel, and to become "all things to all men," (1 Cor. 9:22) even the fifth generation Christian wives should wear the *pottu*.

In North India, I have seen even several Muslim women keeping both sindhur and tilak (*pottu*/bindi). If an alternate cultural style rises just for the sake of fashion, it is a different issue. But in the name of gospel and Christ, what they call (removing the *pottu* and *thali*) as an alternate culture is nothing but imposing their own (Western) ways on the new converts. It is a great tragedy of (Indian) Christianity that all the time only the new converts are expected to adjust themselves according to the conveniences (not even for some biblical conviction) of the traditional Christians, even at the cost of losing their social identity and security. Ignoring the biblical pattern of "becoming all things to all men," (1 Cor. 9:22) the Christians are not ready to crucify their carnal worldviews for the sake of Christ and His gospel.

Idolatry

A positive approach is the best way to prepare a person to receive the truth. Any negative approach will predispose our hearers' minds against us because they will first see more of our religious prejudice than the truth in our message. They may hear what we say but will not pay much attention or truly listen to the truth. I still remember an incident that happened in my own life while I was studying in high school. For three years I attended the Sunday classes and even church service along with my "Christian" friend. After three years, one day he said that all the gods that I worship were fallen angels and devils. Finished! That one negative statement was enough for me to stop going to the Sunday classes. Because the only thought that came to my mind was "All my gods are devils, and his god alone is a true God? Then I don't want such a god." I have yet to find one genuine conversion due to a negative approach.

Preparing a person according to his own understanding is one thing, and criticizing or condemning him for what he does not understand is quite another. Of course, we cannot deny the fact that even in our positive approach sometimes we have to clearly point out lack of understanding and errors. However here also, we must be as polite and humble as possible rather than demonstrating our supposedly superior position. As love alone should be the criteria in all our communication, hurting others' sentiments in any way will not serve our purpose.

The worst offenses in this area are, of course, the Christian denunciations of idol worship that are still too frequently heard and read. Criticism of idol worship seems still the one point of reference for most evangelicals in sharing the gospel. Even when the criticisms are made in sugar–coated words, the approach is still negative which the audience will easily pick up. But there is no need to criticize or condemn idolatry. We can merely say that "It helped you in preparing you to begin your spiritual journey.

Now as you have begun your search for the truth, you must go more and more into your inner being to prepare yourself to receive the truth." This is what I shared with Sri R. A. Dube of Rewa (in M.P.). After he saw for two days the way I silently read the Bible and the way I meditate and pray, he automatically said that he too would gradually stop idol worship. In response to it, instead of condemning idol worship by pointing out all the negative points in it, I said, "That is good. So far it prepared you. Now once you have decided to go further, then you have to set it aside." This helped us to enter into dialogue in the next few days, step by step – each dialogue giving me clear opportunities to share the gospel.

It is best not to talk about idol worship in our initial evangelistic encounters with Hindus. It is a complicated topic, and unless we know what all Hinduism and the Bible say about it, we will end up in mere argument and criticism. In fact, no religion condemns idol worship more than some of the condemnations from within Hinduism. We can quote from every corner of Hinduism, including the *Srimad Bhagavatam* (the classic Krishna text).[56] Simply quoting a few verses from the Old Testament will not help any Hindu and may cause unnecessary offense. To a typical Hindu, all the "names and forms" (*nama-rupa*) representing the invisible God are idols. When the Bible talks about Jesus as the "image of God" it uses the word icon, which actually fits this Hindu concept, wherein Jesus also could be considered an idol. But I have not yet done a proper study on this complex and interesting subject.[57]

This positive approach we are discussing is easy when sharing the gospel by words. However, it becomes more complicated when we build deep relationships with Hindus. There our approach is not limited to verbal communication, but also involves our very practical life. This practical life not only deals with the way we live but how we build up our relationships with them. For those who either live or serve in "compound Christianity" situations, building relationships is not even a consideration. Here, people are culturally and socially cut off from the mainstream of the society, involved only in *kabaddi* evangelism. They either bring the Hindus to their compound to share their faith, or touch them quickly and return safely back to their compound without any moral obligation on their part to develop relationships with others. Such *kabaddi* evangelists find it easy to judge others, particularly those who get involved in incarnational methods of evangelism in building up relationships with others.

As far as the *kabaddi* evangelists are concerned, every effort by the "incarnationalists" is nothing but compromise and syncretism. With such an attitude, it becomes impossible for new believers to stay in their home environment. As a result, the discipleship strategy of the *kabaddi* evangelist is to make every new believer into a full time worker. Conversely, full time ministry is not the solution for any problem, particularly for those who face problems while living as witnesses for Christ in their own homes.[58]

For those who adopt the incarnational method of ministry (both missionaries and Hindu *bhaktas* of Christ) and move beyond the simplistic issues like the red dot, there is still generally a lot of mental and spiritual tension present in relation to involvement in the Hindu *samskaras* (ceremonies). To what extent can a disciple of Christ participate in the socio–religious rituals of their family and friends? Can a new believer marry a non–believer arranged by his family members? What shall a new believer do in the case of his responsibility for performing final rites at the death of his father? What is the appropriate response to the myriad Hindu festivals and the regular sharing of *prasad* brought from the presence of an idol? These crucial issues must be briefly addressed.

There is a simplistic answer often given, saying that all involvement with such Hindu rituals should be avoided, and the rejection that certainly follows is the price one has to pay for his faith. However, this is shortsighted. I may be ready to pay any cost for my faith, but what about the problems created unnecessarily for other members in my family, to whom I should be a loving witness? Those coming from compound Christianity and non–upper castes perhaps will not understand this problem. When I received a letter addressed to S. Christopher Kumar (my previous name, wrongly given to me by Christians), c/o Sambamurthy Iyer, my parents faced several problems in the locality in which they lived. They were mocked and joked at by the other Brahmins, which finally forced them to move their residence. I know that some might jump and shout, "Praise the Lord for such a witness for Christ." On the contrary, this is not a witness as it never gave any opportunity to share the gospel to anyone there.

Prasad (food offered to idols)

Let us see how the early church handled such issues, seeking basic biblical principles. Often what we find in scripture is more in the line of suggestions than commandments, and making some rigid, clear–cut policies will not serve our purpose. One crucial issue will be used as an example; can a Christian accept the *prasad* offered to idols? The *kabaddi* evangelists can stand on a clear cut policy and say "no." Even full– time workers using an "incarnational" approach can usually manage without any difficulties to make a firm decision and politely and positively say "no." But what about those who have to live in their own home and be a witness for Christ?

Simply giving a common solution based on 1 Cor. 10 will only show our lack of proper understanding both of the problem and of the Bible. Anyone who carefully reads the Bible will find that Paul, while writing the epistles in dealing with the local problems of the respective groups, hardly ever quoted from the sayings of Jesus. To say in other words, he never quoted Jesus' words as "the" solution to any particular problem, and in fact, rather rarely quoted from either Jesus or the Old Testament. (I would go to a bit of an extreme and say that Paul was not biblical in the sense that evangelicals often use that word "biblical." He used his insight, reason, and intuition guided by sound teaching and the God–given Spirit to find solutions to local problems rather than merely referring to the Old Testament or the church oral tradition, which was current in his time. Therefore, the claims of some to be "biblical" really amount to "unbiblical.")

Our present day problem and that of the early church may be one and the same. But even in such a case, the social context in which those problems arose was definitely different. Denying such historical context and simply applying that solution to our present situation will not be valid or helpful. The spirit in which Paul and others dealt with those problems is much more important than the actual solution they gave. In the case of Naaman (2 Kings 5), the solution that he got is not so important as the spirit in which Elisha gave it. As he understood Naaman's problem, he said, "Go in peace." In the case of Paul, he was most concerned about the spiritual life of his converts, yet at the same time in their social relationships, he did not want to trouble them beyond what they could bear (I Cor. 5:9–11).[59]

Now coming to details of the issue of the *prasad* offered to idols, note first that the religious context of idol worship is different between Hinduism and the Greek world, though idolatry is always a sin against God. There does not seem to be anything in the Greek traditions that compares to the *prasad* that is present in Hindu traditions. Now when a Hindu offers *prasad* to any one, particularly to any non–Hindu, what is he thinking and what is his motive? Generally when offered *prasad*, Christians immediately want to refuse to accept it, and if the situation permits, also to explain their convictions. But have we even ever asked why he is giving it to us? For a typical Hindu, *prasad* means God's grace, and as he received it, now he has a moral obligation to share it with everyone. He cannot keep it or enjoy God's grace for himself alone. And when he shares the *prasad,* his aim is not to convert others (particularly non–Hindus) to his faith, nor is he silently enjoying a thought that he is causing others to compromise. While distributing the *prasad*, he will not even enquire about the others' faith. Yet, we will refuse it because of our conscience, which always invariably links religious activity with proselytizing efforts.

Whenever the Christians share the gospel, their main motive is to proselytize others to their "religion," viz., to Christianity. They then see their neighbors of other faiths through the prism

of their own narrow perspective with all their religious prejudices and complex feelings. Therefore, when a Hindu comes and
shares his *prasad*, even though he is without any such motive to
convert others to his faith, yet because of their guilty conscience,
Christians refuse it. However, his conscience is completely clear.
His aim is not to convert, but only to share God's grace. Even if
you want to become a Hindu, he neither wants you to become a
Hindu nor can allow you to become a Hindu. Because you can
never "become" a Hindu, but can only be "born" as a Hindu.

So keeping this understanding, when a Hindu offers any
kind of *prasad*, there is no reason to refuse. But after accepting
it, when a proper relationship has been established, with much
humility and love, it can be made clear to him that your conviction (religious?) is actually against accepting the *prasad* offered
to an idol. Furthermore, you can clearly show to him that the
prasad that was accepted was accepted not as a *prasad* of god,
but as a *prasad* (grace) of his own love. When approaching this
issue in such a positive way, the Hindu will not bring any more
prasad, because a Hindu almost invariably respects the others'
religious sentiments more than a non–Hindu does.

Now in the context in which Paul deals with the issue of
food offered to idols (1 Cor. 10), it clearly says that the criteria
about deciding to receive *prasad* is the conscience of both sides.
Here, however, the conscience of the giver is not clearly defined,
whether it refers to his giving it to convert you to his faith, etc.
Besides, it is very difficult to predict what would have been
the "conscience" of the Greek pagans behind offering to his
neighbor who now follows Jesus any *prasad* offered to his gods.
Whatever it may be, here in India, we know clearly the mind or
conscience of our Hindu neighbor. Now accepting or rejecting it
depends upon our conscience as well as our commitment to the
Lord. By accepting such *prasad*, if a Christian feels that his faith
will be at stake or his commitment will be disturbed or even if
he has some fear of power encounter, then he has every right to
refuse it. However, in my last twenty years as a *bhakta* of Jesus,

I never faced any problem nor has my Hindu neighbor ever felt that he has won me back to his faith.

Nevertheless, the question of our weak brother's conscience is always raised. But again the differing contexts of the New Testament, and today, must be fully accounted for. The weak brother in the New Testament was one who might mix up discipleship to Jesus on the one hand and idolatry on the other, upon seeing my "enlightened" practice of eating what was offered to idols. But today, it is invariably the problem that the "weak brother" is a Christian who gets annoyed at seeing what he believes to be compromise. Such a person is never tempted to worship idols, so we need not fear causing him to stumble in the biblical sense. He needs more understanding, and we must strengthen his personal faith and commitment to the Lord rather than preventing him from building up his relationships with others. How long he is going to remain weak? Teach him and strengthen him, and if he remains unteachable in this area, then simply ignore him.

If one calls this syncretism, then we have to say that Paul himself was such a syncretist when it came to building up his relationships with the Jews. Leaving Acts 16:3 (which seems a total contradiction to the decision taken unanimously based on the issue that Paul himself had brought before the council in Acts 15) and Acts 18:18, just take Acts 21:21–26. What Paul has done here is what we are doing with our own people. Here Paul's aim is not to convince the Jewish Christians, but to win back his own unbelieving Jews. How far he was successful is not our question, but what we see here is his spirit of building up his relationships with his own people. What Paul has done as a Jew is what we are doing as Hindus. If he were here in India, he would have done the same thing. Similarly, in the other issue of circumcision, he never allowed the Gentile converts to become Jews, nor stopped the Jews from remaining Jews.

Idol worship is a sin against God. However, our attitude and approach should be positive. Mere criticism may help to win an argument, but it will not help to win that person. Particularly new converts who have to live in their own homes, and more specifically girls and women who cannot be pulled out for a "full–time job" (not "ministry"), must be sympathetically encouraged to be witnesses at home. There our attitude should be that of Elisha towards Naaman rather than that of the Pharisees towards the woman caught in adultery (who were ready to punish the victim rather than the criminals who used her (John 8:3–11)). Any hasty decision to pull such people out from their situations and to transplant them into a "Christian" environment in order to prevent their taking part in certain religious rituals will permanently close the door in that community for sharing the gospel. Such a transplanted new believer, however much receiving initial moral support, love, care and concern among the Christians, will in the long run be psychologically affected. His desire to have fellowship with his own people cannot be substituted for by any amount of shifting concerns from the Christians. Since the last 20 years, my brother has stopped talking with me, and others cannot understand my emotional problems once I ran away from my home. Particularly for every Hindu convert, however modern he may become (even Western), lack of cultural identity and community relationship will create some kind of unrecognized and incommunicable psychological problem.

Marriage

Honor your father and mother is the first commandment with a promise (Eph. 6:2). Can we honor that command in faithfulness to Christ when issues of marriage and funeral rites arise? No outsider, however spiritual he may be, has the right to arbitrarily make any final pronouncement on such questions. He can guide and pray and support and encourage, but has no right to sit in judgment (Rom. 14:4). Each individual is a person, and we must respect his personality. No matter how much Christians emphasize corporate worship and witness, yet they have no right to interfere in the community life of a Hindu. Those who are cut off from the social mainstream of Indian life cannot understand the rigid community life of a Hindu (note that Christian caste communities and denominational church communities are in no way better in several "rigid" community norms of their own). Particularly those Christians who have become Western oriented do not understand the integral fabric of a Hindu community where cultural, social and religious aspects are inter–mingled. Simply defining certain cultural and social activities as religious ones will only reveal our lack of understanding of the issues.

Notice that when Paul was dealing with the marriage and divorce issues between believers and non–believers, he did not directly quote from either Jesus' teachings or from the Old Testament, but deals with that particular situation in the Gentile world. We too must follow him. Each situation demands its own interpretation of biblical principles, never exhausting or denying the basic truth. We cannot give any one, permanent solution as each individual and situation deserves its own treatment. We should first seek the spirit with which such problems were dealt with in that given situation. Not rigid rules but understanding and a sympathetic spirit is the way to move toward solutions in all these issues. May God help us all to gain the same "spirit" of Christ, which is seen in Matthew 11:28–30, 12:19–20.

In India, marriage is not just the right of a boy or girl, but it is the social responsibility of his and her parents. This even goes for the tribal Christians and "down south" Christians [those from the most Christian district in south India at the very southern point of the peninsula]. Even among the educated people love marriages, particularly with another caste, are hardly encouraged as they affect the family prestige. Children who choose their own marriage partner are acting without concern for their culture and invariably displease their parents, which is a clear violation of biblical commands. The arranged marriage system is not perfect, but it is certainly not against any biblical truth and gives children an opportunity to honor and submit to their parents. Accordingly, when the parents of a believer arrange the marriage with an unbeliever, the boy/girl has to obey them.

Quoting 2 Cor. 6:14–15 is of no use here. First, note that in the whole book of 2 Corinthians, nowhere does Paul deal with marriage, and so these verses cannot be directly applied to this area. Just taking the word "yoke" and imposing marriage on that word is a false interpretation. Paul's direct teaching on marriage is in First Corinthians chapter seven. There, Paul's instruction about the marriage of a widow is that it is to be with a "believer." Because being a widow, now she is free and no more under the direct control of her parents. As a result, she should select a husband who belongs to the Lord. Whereas, in the case of boys and girls who are living with their parents, it is necessary to obey their parents. Should we not have faith, knowing that God is in absolute control and can overrule the parents for the sake of His child whose life is committed to His care? We can give several examples from the lives of converts who were blessed with suitable partners because of their trust in God and obedience to their parents. Of course in the case of an individual having a choice, they are to marry "in the Lord."

The common saying that unbelieving spouses will make the believing spouses go back to their Hindu faith is a poor understanding. Then what about their faith in Christ? Why can they not win the other spouse because of their life and witness? Marriage is a serious issue in India, and disobeying the parents may permanently close the door in that family for the gospel. A male convert, mostly after coming for so–called full–time ministry, can boldly marry a Christian girl. Ramesh was a new convert. The first concern of his parents was clear when they asked him to promise, before me, that he would never marry a "dummy Christian girl" (his father's own words). Conversely, what about the girls who cannot run away from home in the name of full–time ministry?

Further, there is no guarantee that people are going to remain faithful to Christ till the end just because their partner is a believer. Their partner may help or hinder growth to a limited extent only. Finally, it is based on personal conviction rather than on a partner's. If you quote King Solomon, from the Old Testament, for the backsliding of a husband from the faith because of his wives, I can give a number of cases where the partner has won the other because of their faith in Christ. It is better to trust

God and marry an unbeliever, than to disobey parents and be a stumbling block for them to come to Christ. In India, marriage is a social and family issue rather than a personal affair. Even in one very wealthy family, one person finally committed suicide because the whole family opposed his marriage and even practically ran after him to separate him from his wife.

If marriage with a believer approved by the parents can be arranged, this is clearly the best option. However, in arranging such a marriage, is it necessary for it to take place inside a church building? Particularly for new believers Western dress, a band, a cake, and a veil for the bride are completely unnecessary. Even Christian marriages arranged inside the church are really "secular" marriages. A pastor, without holding the marriage license from the secular government, cannot perform the marriage. Whereas in the Hindu society, if a marriage is just witnessed by the relatives and friends, even performed without any religious ceremony, it becomes legal.

S. P. Singh of Kanpur, with the permission of his parents arranged his marriage with a Christian believer outside the church according to his family customs (like touching the parents' feet, exchanging garlands and putting *sindur* as a mark of marriage, etc.) which saved his parents' prestige in his community and is now helping him to witness to them along with his wife, who is happily accepted by them. Recently, one CSI pastor arranged his marriage in St. George's Cathedral in Chennai in exactly the South Indian way – in dress, decoration, music, etc. The reporter of *Anandavikadan* (A Tamil weekly magazine) asked about this at the bridegroom's house and they said, "Even though we are staunch Christians, yet we are Tamilians also, so we desired to conduct the marriage in our Tamilian way. For this, we removed the old British traditions and found the Tamil traditions and used them." The surprise in it is that the bridegroom, Sri Preme, is a theological graduate and the bride's father is also a pastor. May the other Christians in India also catch the same vision!

Subramanian Raman (a leading table tennis player and Arjuna Award winner) and his wife Bhuvana (also a nationally recognized table tennis player, both are believers and from a Brahmin community) were confused and (mis)guided by some Christians who insisted that they should only marry in the church otherwise they would not be

witnessing for the Lord to their family. However, another friend and I met with them and cleared up some of their doubts. Finally, they agreed to marry according to their family tradition. One small ritual (wearing the thread by Raman) was performed by me using Bible verses (in Sanskrit), and both their families were happy as their family prestige (before their relatives and community), and particularly Bhuvana's father's right to "give" his daughter in marriage, were preserved. Now they have good relationships with their parents and relatives, and this opened several opportunities to have dialogue with them in a meaningful way. Interestingly, both parents knew of their faith in Christ and were ready to go to any extent to cut short on rituals in order to accommodate their faith. The parents' main point was that arranging the marriage was their right and duty (as a social obligation), arranging the marriage inside the church would deprive them of their right. They had no problem with their children's faith in Christ but only against their marriage inside the church – as such a marriage is considered both Western as well as outside their community.

Finally, let me note that in personal talks several believers have accepted the fact that in marriage, faith does not help much because marriage is something both husband and wife have to work out based on human relationships. Of course in a believer's life his/her faith will help him/her to co–operate more, but in spite of their faith, marriage is something to be worked out based on mutual commitment, love and respect. That is why in spite of their faith, several believers' marriages ended in divorce. Above all, if "faith" is the only criteria in a believer's marriage, then most of the marriages arranged among the traditional Christians are unbiblical, since in most cases marriage is arranged based on their own convenience (based on caste, etc.) rather than on faith. The familiar A,B,C of Christian marriage is: A for ability, B for beauty, C for caste, D for dowry, E for

education, F for family and finally G for God (often not the
faith in God of a "born again believer" but simply having faith
in their "Christian God" is enough). Of course one mistake
cannot justify another mistake, but before trying to remove
the "speck" from another's eye one should try to remove the
"plank" from one's own (Matt. 7:5). So instead of judging a
Hindu Christ *bhakta*'s marriage, they should have a proper understanding about their own situation, equally accepting their
own plight in this area.

Funeral Rites

In a Hindu community, one can avoid participating in a marriage function for any genuine reason, but no reason is acceptable for missing the funeral of a near relative. Particularly if a
son (for any reason whatever) refuses to do the final rights of his
father, not only will he be cut of from his family and community, but he will not inherit any of his father's property. This being
the case, every Hindu "convert" is in double danger of losing his
ancestral property; first for his "conversion" and second for not
performing the final rites of his father.

As in the case of other *samskaras,* the Bible is silent about a
believer participating or performing the final rites for his father.
Christians, having all kinds of social security, have no right to
prevent a "convert" from performing this ceremony by saying
that God will doubly compensate all his loss for the sake of his
faith. It is true that those who for the sake of Jesus and the gospel are denied everything will receive fathers, mothers, brothers,
and sisters here and eternal life hereafter. But here, the context
is rather different. Likewise, if a "convert" is thrown away from
his family and community because of his faith, then he can do
nothing but keep away from all kinds of final rites. However,
our entire context is about those Christ *bhaktas* who are witnessing within their family and community. Thus, all that we said
about marriage and taking *prasad* is also applicable here.

Just for the sake of property, a disciple of Christ cannot
perform the final rites; but because of his filial relationship and
above all for the sake of the gospel, he must go the second mile.

Imagine the case of a *bhakta* of Christ who is living as a witness in his own family and community when his father dies. He, as the only son, should perform the final rites. If he refuses this role, how will his mother, sisters and other relatives view his faith in Christ? They will all think that following Christ means he has to deny not only his filial responsibility, but he is also depriving his father's own birthright (as his father has the right to receive final rites from his son).[60] No amount of explanation about his faith and doctrines will convince his mother and other relatives that he can be excused; and a time of grief is not an appropriate time for a theological discussion. So for the sake of the gospel, he must perform the final rites for his father.

There are innumerable varieties of rituals performed in Hindu funeral ceremonies, but most are actually done by the officiating priest. The rituals have little theological meaning and with *mantras* all chanted in Sanskrit, no one generally knows what is going on. It is not a worship or teaching service by which one is compromised if participating. Death ceremonies are a social event, and lack of participation does not communicate theological conviction but rather social belligerence. The mourning period which follows certainly does not entail compromise of biblical convictions. The shaving of the head or the wearing of white clothes after the death of a relative is only a sign of mourning and has nothing to do with any deity or philosophy. Therefore, every believer has the right to participate in the mourning of his relatives, particularly that of his parents.

Many of the points above related to *prasad*, marriage and funeral rites have been vehemently criticized by several evangelical Christians. Some even said that I am the promoter of a new cult within Christianity, and all that I share is nothing but heresy. One even commented that what I am promoting is nothing but "Christo–paganism." But for me it is better to be a heretic and love the Lord than to be a fanatic and become a Pharisee. While new believers have generally been found faithfully promoting their faith in their own way among their own people, only the established church was busy with promoting all kinds of heresy, as well described by Roland Allen :

> The great heresies in the early church arose not from the rapid expansion resulting from the work of these unknown teachers, but in those churches which were longest established, and where the Christians were not so busily engaged in converting the heathen round them....The danger to the doctrine lay not in these illiterate converts on the outskirts; but at home, in places like Ephesus and Alexandria, amongst the more highly educated and philosophically minded Christians. It was against them that she had to maintain the doctrine.[61]

New Names

"Therefore, if any one is in Christ, he is a new creation; the old has gone, the new has come!" (2 Cor. 5:17) The first new thing that comes because of a Hindu's faith in Christ is a new name given by the Christians. Even in giving a new name, they give strange European – Greek – Hebrew names which most of the new converts, particularly those from uneducated backgrounds, have to struggle just to remember. This is an aspect of Christian Pharisaism that is completely without biblical or practical defense.

A missionary named Wilson, himself a convert who attained the new name of "Wilson," said that because he does not want to pronounce the name of other gods (Ps. 16:4), he changed the name of his convert from Krishna to Robert. When I asked what is the meaning of "Wilson" and "Robert," he said that he did not know. Then I drew his attention to the "pagan" names in the Bible, like Titus (it is also the name of the Roman commander who destroyed the Jerusalem temple in A. D. 70), Timothy, Luke, Lydia, etc. Paul never changed his converts' names. Who knows, if we trace the origin of European and Greek names, they may be the names of some "pagan" deities in their countries, as is the case regarding the great NT preacher Apollos. Also, the "biblical" name Asenath, which some Christians give to their daughters, is completely pagan. Asenath means "she belongs to Neith," a goddess of the Egyptians.[62]

The common claim that "Saul" became "Paul" is almost surely not true. The Bible does not suggest that Saul became Paul in the sense that he attained a new name. Being a citizen of Rome, he might have had the Greek name of Paul all his life, and being a strong advocate of identification would have switched from his Hebrew name Saul to the Greek name Paul during his Gentile ministry. In Acts 13:2 we see that he could still be called Saul, which is a strong argument for his having had two names.

No Hindu ever remembers the gods when they call another person with such names as Rama (pleasant one) or Krishna (black), though they may indeed have been named after the deity. Even if we take it for granted that they are repeating their gods' names by calling others by such names, then does it mean that they are actually scolding or threatening their gods when they do it with a person called Rama or Krishna? When they say, "Rama is dead" does it mean that their god Rama is dead? If merely calling a person by his name means addressing their gods, then we even have to change or give a new name for Sunday, Monday, etc., as they are the name of deities in almost every language. "These new (Christian?) names stand as a witness for our Lord," some argue. Then what about smugglers, kidnappers, murderers, drug traffickers and prostitutes with "Christian" names?

After his conversion, P. K. Ramesh, an 18 year–old Brahmin boy, shared his new faith with his parents, telling them that he had officially become a Christian now and was baptized. Therefore, he was no longer Palakadu Krishnamoorty (his father's name) Ramesh, but had now become "Paul Krupakaran" Ramesh. When I later met his father in my mission of reconciliation to take him back to his home (as he had run away), I saw his father's reaction and anger. Ramesh's father was deeply hurt and no amount of my words could convince him. "By changing my name for someone else's," he said, "how he has disgraced his mother." Every evangelist should have to personally face the ramifications of changing names to help them understand and change their view on this topic. Such unnecessary "Christian" activity becomes a stumbling block and closes the door in others' hearts and minds once and for all against the gospel. My parents faced a lot of problems because of my "Christian" name of Christopher. Do not say that it was a witness for Christ when in fact it was a stumbling block to my parents, who began to hate even the word "Christian" because of that.

I once met a south Indian (Tamil) boy named Billy Graham. Without any surprise, I asked the reason for keeping a Western name. "Billy Graham himself gave me that name," was the reply. "Great," I said. "Why could Billy Graham not have thought of giving at least some Jewish or Greek name from the Bible to a south Indian? Why this American name?" I know of a Sri William F. Stapleton, an American, who became "Tamatsukuri" in Japan and another American became Gurmit Singh in India for the sake of Christ; but a south Indian is "Billy Graham" in India! "God forgive them for they know not what they are doing."

While we are giving Greek, Roman, and Jewish names to the new converts in the name of giving them biblical names, Bruce Olson gives an interesting record of giving new names to Bible characters:

> The Motilone, for instance, always use names that have a meaning. There are no names like Kent or Kim that are names and nothing more. So Bible characters had to be given names that made sense. Abraham became the "Man Who Knows God," John the Baptist became the "Announcer" and "Jungle Dweller," and Jesus "The only Son of God with Us." Every time a name had to be given, we spent long hours around the fire discussing the person and what kind of a name would be best for him. Often other Motilones would join us and would help with the decision.[63]

So in the name of sharing the gospel, we should not do anything that will upset the basic social fabric of the society. As Olsen says, "No good news should tear their social system into shreds."[64]

G. IN RELATING TO THE INDIAN NATION

Patriotism is not narrow–mindedness, and remaining loyal to one's own country is not unbiblical. Generally Indian Christians tend to divide life into several watertight compartments and try to live each part independently. For example, the three hours worship inside the church building is one compartment, and the life outside it for the rest of the six days and 21 hours are other compartments. That is why they used to say "I am first a Christian and then an Indian." But they forget that

> Dedication to the Christian faith does not, in any way, detract from devotion and loyalty to the country, for *one can be authentically Christian and authentically Indian at one and the same time.* The apparent conflict between being a "Christian" and being an "Indian" arose from historic reasons. There has been a traditional notion that Christianity is of Western origin and it has been imported into India. Secondly, under British rule, when there occurred an impact of Western thought and culture on India, more precise, the church in India, *let itself be converted into a tool of the alien rulers* (sic). In the socio–cultural field, there were three distinct types of reaction to the impact of Western ideas: (i)The extreme orthodox refused to contaminate their ideas with the Western ideas. (ii) A second section was almost infatuated with Western ideals. (iii) The renascent thinkers, who constituted a "creative minority," accepted the west and assimilated the best in it.[65]

Most Indian Christians belong to the second type. Conversely, in the area of patriotism, they are not following their Western directors. I have been told that in the Methodist denomination in America, churches keep both the church and national flags inside the church. Reportedly, in some high Anglican churches in the USA, they keep the national flag above the pulpit. The Norwegian believers celebrate their national days with much pride and joy. One American young man living at Lucknow gave treats to others on the July 4th to celebrate his Independence Day. While I was sharing among the I.I.T. students in Madras, during question hour in way of answer to a question on persecution, I asked, "How many of your churches celebrate Independence day?" One M. Tech. student replied, "We are Christians so why should we celebrate Independence day?" "Then," I said, "You Christians deserve to be persecuted."

It is particularly sad that Christians in India simply blame Hindu nationalists without making any efforts to prove their own national spirit. Though Christians may have a true national spirit, yet in India it is not expressed properly. Recently I spoke with an editor of a leading English Newspaper, himself a "Hindu convert to Christianity," who said, "It is not right to have patriotism or nationalism in our Christian faith as our faith is beyond all this." This is a prime example of the compartmentalizing that goes on.

Another example of our lack of patriotism happened in a leadership training center where they also have a high school. While the high school students were singing the National Anthem, the leadership trainees came out of the dining hall after the tea break. Except for a few of us, no one paid any attention to the National Anthem and most just went on walking and talking. Several of them were missionaries from the field who had come there for a refresher course. The next day in the dining hall, during the announcement time, after mentioning this incident, the director said, "In order to give respect to our National Anthem, we have requested the school authorities to sing the National Anthem either before or after our tea time." What a shame for us.

During the last 20 years as a *bhakta* of Christ, I have never witnessed any Christian meetings or conferences ending with the singing of the National Anthem. Please do not misunderstand me. I think that Christians should not ask, "Do they (Hindus) sing the National Anthem at the end of their religious meetings?" because Christians cannot always lead a life of comparison with the Hindus. My point is that a true disciple of Christ can never divide his life as secular, spiritual, social and religious, etc.[66] For us, every area of our life is "spiritual." This does not mean that I will say that at the end of each church service they should sing the National Anthem. No! But when the Christians gather for missionary conferences, meetings, etc. why should they not occasionally sing our National Anthem at the end of the conference after final prayer and benediction?

I took my own advice at a recent teaching ministry with a Christian group at Bangalore. After my final message, prayer and benediction, I requested that all the brothers stand up to sing our National Anthem, and they all happily cooperated. However, at the same time, nearly 15 CSI pastors and a few Baptist missionaries, who had come there for another meeting, were playing volleyball. When they heard the National Anthem, a few out of curiosity only turned their heads toward the meeting hall (probably they were hearing it for the first time in their life in a Christian meeting!) but none of them stopped playing to stand at attention – just for two minutes, the time it takes for us to sing our National Anthem. They continued their play and all of them are mainline church pastors and missionaries.

A similar incident happened on Independence Day, 15th August 1992. I was in a Christian compound in the north. There were nearly 20 people there and all of them were Indians, but nothing was arranged to celebrate Independence Day. Because I was a guest, I could only gently point it out but not force them to make any arrangements to hoist the flag and celebrate the day. Regarding celebrating national days in the church, one Methodist pastor objected and said, "Church is a place for worship and not for politics. We need not and cannot hoist any flag there." In the same way while I was sharing on the same point with a group of Indian missionaries one said, "Even our Prime Minister (then Sri N. Rao) says that we must keep politics away from the religion, whereas you ask us to celebrate Independence Day by hoisting the national flag on the church premises?"

On hearing such comments, though not surprised, I do not know whether to laugh or weep. All these incidents only show the general trend among Indian Christians and reveals the way they were brought up inside their churches. For them, celebrating Independence Day and hoisting the national flag become politics! Even a missionary and a pastor do not seem to understand that the national flag and National Anthem are not any symbol of politics. Though "we cannot judge any community on the basis of a few members of that community," yet the average Christian in India does not seem to know where politics ends and where nationalism or patriotism begins.

Another Christian leader raised his objection by saying, "Do they (Hindus) hoist the national flag in their temples?" My answer is "Why should they hoist the flag in their temple?" For a Hindu, the temple is the dwelling place of his god and he goes there for his personal *sadhana* [devotional exercises].[67]

As the Bible tells us in Acts 17:24, the Lord does not live in temples made by hands. Even the concept of a church building as a worshipping place is extra–biblical and imposed upon us by tradition.[68] The church in the New Testament meaning is not a worshipping place but a witnessing community. But nowadays it has often become a mere social club, taking care of "hatch," "match" and "dispatch" of her members. It has lost the vitality and understanding of New Testament times.

Apart from this, a Hindu is not under an obligation to prove his patriotism. Only Muslims and Christians (with rare exceptions) behave as if they have nothing to do with the welfare of this country. A Hindu will not say, as most Christians will, that first he is a Hindu and then an Indian. Because every Indian is a Hindu and every Hindu is an Indian, because the word "Hindu" is more related to the geographical identity of the people than with anyone's personal religious allegiance. The Hindus never gather in their temples to witness to outsiders but to perform their own personal religious rituals and *sadhana* for their spiritual progress. As a result, this is not only a poor comparison but a wrong one.

The attitudes reflected in the examples above are not just individual opinions but reflect the community in which these people were born and brought up. Christianity not only came in Western garb but still remains in it. Many Christians, even today, glorify British rule and remain loyal to it in their spirit, forgetting the fact that, "the pride of Lucifer before the Creator was nothing compared to the arrogance of the English before history." [69]

Though a few Christians participated in the Independence movement, most remained aloof. In south India particularly, when we hear about V. O. Chidembaram Pillai, Subramaniya Siva, Bharatiyar, Vancinathan and others connected with the Independence struggle, we hardly hear about the participation of any Indian Christians. (As the Western missionaries decided to keep neutral, naturally they never encouraged Indian Christians to take an active part in the Independence struggle. But neutrality sometimes becomes more dangerous than taking part with one side.) On the other hand, those few Christians who showed national spirit were often carefully avoided by the church (like R. C. Das, Brahmabandab Upadhyay, etc.).

Missionary compromises with imperialism are clearly documented by Elizabeth Susan Alexander in her study of Madras Presidency in the 1920s. She shows how:

> Missionaries expressed any criticism of the British Government's actions, with great caution. In 1919, most missionaries who expressed their criticism of the British Government authorities' actions in the Punjab, including the Jallianwala Bagh massacre, reserved their opinions until the publication of the Official Enquiry Commission's report on the issue, which also found fault with British official actions. Many missionaries who criticized the timing or provisions of the Reform Act of 1919 were decidedly circumspect and diplomatic in their criticism. That missionaries at times criticized Government measures such as those take by Gen. Dyer in Amritsar in 1919, as being "un–English," only endorses the fact that missionaries had, basically, firm faith in the goodness of the British.

> These obvious trends in missionary attitudes heightened the identification of Christian missionaries with the British Establishment in India, in the mind of most Indians.[70]

Thankfully some missionaries sided with India, such as Stanley Jones who was banned from entering the country due to his widely known sympathy with the freedom fighters. Most Christians followed the feeble example of the majority of missionaries, but thankfully, there were also exceptions. A striking case study is of Dr. Savarirayan Yesudasan of Kristukula Ashram of Tiruppatur, who wrote the book *Daivabhaktiyum Desabhaktiyum* (Devotion to God and Patriotism) in 1931. He relates how "When last year one devoted Christian student joined the *Satyagraha* struggle and went to jail, one Christian pastor with much contempt told to me, 'I cannot understand how a Christian can get involved in such activity.'" [71]

This is not just past history because, as Selvanayagam has observed, "Compared to the political witness of a few Christians before independence in not only taking active part in the national movement but also acting as peace makers at times of Hindu–Muslim conflict, the present generation of Christians looks so introverted and selfish, being passive at times of conflict and thus losing their credibility." [72]

Wherever the gospel goes, it makes changes and brings definite distinctions in society, but it never abolishes or rejects those aspects of national life on which the Bible remains silent. The only distinction that outsiders witnessed among the early believers was, according to the famous historian Gibbon, "how they love each other." But in India, Christians seem to be lacking in love for each other and for outsiders and for their nation. Like an average Hindu, who does not know much of history, Indian Christians seem to get confused about British rule and the service of the Christian missionaries.

"But for the British rule, India would never be a country as it is at present on the world map," argue most Christians. But remember that it was not British rule which gave this political unity of India as one country, but rather it was the Congress leaders in raising the national spirit by opposing the British rule. The well–known policy of the British was "divide and rule." [73] Moreover, they never wished to leave a united India even after Independence. The partition creating Pakistan is a tragedy, for which we are still paying a huge price today. Even the Hyderabad Nizam was brought under Indian rule by Sardar Patel. Because when the British left India, they left Hyderabad as an independent state within India. When the British government left India, she left an empty treasury with lots of problems for us to face.[74]

India became one country politically not because of the good office of British rule but because of our own *spiritual and cultural heritage.* Otherwise, how would both the Hindus and Muslims (though not many Christians) have responded in one spirit (in spite of vast differences), from south to north and east to west, to the call of national leaders to fight against British rule. Of course the spirit of nationalism is a recent development, and India as one nation is also modern. Yet this spirit of nationalism is possible because of the basic spiritual and cultural heritage of many centuries.

When the cord of Communism broke the USSR broke down into 13 republics within a few days, Czechs and Slovaks separated themselves, just as the Bosnians, Croatians and Serbs were fighting with each other. But in spite of ethnic, racial, cultural and even religious differences we Indians remain as one nation not because of political unity (if our country breaks up, it will be due to the greed of our corrupt politicians) but because of our cultural and spiritual heritage. That is why I am an *Indian culturally, socially, politically, spiritually and even religiously* (here referring to *dharma* and not to *sampradaya* which means "sect"); certainly not because of British rule but because *I am an Indian.* That is why I am an Indian *bhakta* of Christ, not first a Christian and then an Indian. Rather *authentically Christ–in and Indian both at one and the same time.*

Regarding the progress that India did receive under the British rule: the British brought some basic things like railway, postal service, education, etc., not keeping the welfare of Indians in mind but to use India for their own welfare. They brought the railways to bring raw materials quickly to the ports, to send them to England and imported the finished products again to send quickly to Indian markets. To quicken communications for business, they brought the postal system. To get local clerks and *babus* education was introduced. If we give all the credit only to British rule in India for any progress we made, then what about those countries the British never ruled, but who became powerful countries more quickly even than England and America, like Japan.

Vishal Mangalwadi is now suggesting that it was not Gandhiji but the gospel which brought independence to India.[75] But even if we take for granted that it is the gospel and not Gandhiji that gave freedom to India, Mangalwadi has to accept that it was not the Christians but only Hindus and Muslims who paid the cost for it. So naturally the question that will arise in the minds of Indians will be, "If the Christian gospel gave freedom and brought development to India, why could it not motivate Christians to participate in the freedom struggle then and nation building now? Above all, if the gospel gave freedom to us, then why can it not give religious freedom to Indian Christians who still remain enslaved to their Western religious system?"

Dr. Yesudasan's book mentioned above shows how the British never did much to benefit India, not even fulfilling its natural duty as ruler. He gives a list of British government expenditure, which I here round off leaving out the quarter and half crore figures:

> Army: 55 crores [ten millions]
> Police and govt. officials: 40 crores
> Pension to the retired British officials: 3 crores
> Govt. Loan: more than 900 crores (which the tax payers alone had to return)

Compare this with the money spent on public welfare:

> All India education: 11 Crores
> Medical: 3 crores
> Sanitation: 2 crores
> Agriculture: 2 crores
> Small scale industries etc.: 1 crore[76]

If you point out the bridges and dams strongly built by the British government, I can equally point out the dam built by the Chola king in Trichy (*Kallanai*) 1,500 years ago, and the *Taj Mahal* by Shajahan and the Golden Temple in Amristar by the Sikhs. I am not denying altogether that some good initiatives were received through British rule, particularly through the influence of missionaries. And at the same time, I am not denying the lack of proper political integrity, honesty and hard work among our present Indian leaders (with every kind of scam under the sun) and people now. In spite of our present weaknesses, we should not glorify the past rule by the British government. In one way, it was because of British rule that we did not make the real progress, which we ought to have made. Because of Pakistan, we are wasting lots of money on defense (more than 3,000 crores in a year!?!) which is due to a British mistake. "Thus the legacy that the British left behind them was the curse of partition." [77]

You are probably wondering why I am sidetracking to spend such a long time complaining about British rule. However, I did this to make the following point. Instead of blaming present India and glorifying past British rule, Christians should involve themselves in the building of the nation by joining the nation's mainstream, even in politics. When most Christians are not even exercising their voting privilege, what right have they to blame our government?

> It is often forgotten that independent India had to start almost from scratch in most fields of development and welfare. Besides, the baby that was Independent India began to toddle on its weak legs and to venture out a few hesitant steps in a situation of utter chaos, caused chiefly by the vivisection of India followed by widespread riots and mass migrations of millions of people, perhaps unprecedented in history on such a large scale. Besides, the fact that India with its 2000 castes, 826 languages and major dialects, and with most of the major religious and racial groups, is still surviving as a unified entity, is no small miracle. In spite of such diversity and such gigantic problems, Indians today constitute almost 50 percent of the people of the world who enjoy democratic freedom, a rare luxury in the Afro—Asian situation.[78]

(For further points see Appendix C: Indianness: What is Wrong?)

Let us show a patriotic spirit. Nationalism is neither un-biblical nor mere narrow mindedness. Organize Independence and Republic Day celebrations in your church and invite your neighbor. As long as you hold Indian citizenship, remain loyal to this country. That many Christians remain loyal to British rule in their mind and spirit and always glorify the past life of slavery under it, deeply hurts a real Indian and closes his heart and mind for the gospel. Let us begin a better pattern of national pride appropriately displayed, as seen in the life of Kalicaran Banerjea more than a century ago, "Kalicaran went on to become not only a leading Churchman but also a prominent national-ist....One of the main aims of Kalicaran's life was to show that one could be a Christian and remain a patriot. In this attempt he was something of a pioneer..." [79]

A closing point must be made in light of Christian emphasis on internationalism. This present trend of internationaliza-tion among big organizations and mission movements serving world—wide should raise serious questions in our minds. It is a good sign that some Western leaders in international organiza-

tions seriously think, talk and take steps to internationalize their
organizations (de–Westernize them). But what causes concern
is that while they try to de–Westernize their movements, they
indirectly impose their Westernization without realizing it. They
may take Indians and Asians into international conclaves, but
those Indians and Asians are often more Westernized than the
Westerners. Furthermore, these Westernized Asians and Indians
may feel at home with their Western counterparts in their organizations, but they often cannot effectively contribute much to
the indigenization of the church and Christian endeavor in their
home country. This may sound like a rather extreme view, but
those who are really involved in such issues with first hand experience of the problem will alone realize what we wish to say. This
is again something already well said in the past, by R. C. Das:

> The greatest damage to the Indian mind, soul and heart has been done
> through Western nationalistic church systems, forms of worship and theo-
> logical studies. The Indian Christian mind has never been allowed to rest
> and pause and think about his own country, its history, literature, philoso-
> phy, faith, customs and manners – its heritage in culture and thought.
>
> Everything in Western art and culture has been exalted. Even the politi-
> cal systems have been borrowed. Internationalism has been exalted over
> nationalism, which has been always decried. By internationalism has been
> meant Western nationalism in fact. Ecumenism is practically meant to be
> the church polity of the West in some form or other. The Indian form
> does not exist yet or is taboo. We can give scores of instances to illustrate
> these points. This process is still going on very rapidly in theological institu-
> tions. A false idea of internationalism and nationalism has been taught to
> spread. Has internationalism any meaningful content without strong and
> living nationalism? Why should Eastern nationalism only be exclusive and
> aggressive? Is not internationalism aggressive and exclusive today? What
> missionaries parade as internationalism is but Western nationalism magni-
> fied and sublimated.[80]

Some Indians and Asians, who are very much involved in this
process of internationalization may be offended by this statement. They will try to prove that they are Indian in every sense,
but they forget their plight, which perhaps they cannot even see
and realize. They may very well live in India and try to remain
Indian even in their outward life style. Nevertheless, their attitude and approach in several areas has become completely

Westernized. However, when we Indians point this out, then the Westernized Indians who are playing an active role in internationalization will say that we are jealous of their position; and if any Westerner points this out, then they (the Westernized Indians) will say that they (such Westerners) actually do not want us (Indians) to share with them because they see us as a threat to their monopoly in the international affairs. But those who really want to see true internationalization will work more towards indigenization than internationalization, especially as the latter is nothing but Westernizing under a different name.

Notes

1   I noted down the quotation from this book in my early days before I worried about writing and references, so cannot now provide proper bibliographical information.

2   I am indebted to Sri V. Thyaharajan for this quote from a Hindu acquaintance of his.

3   *Christ the Controversialist*, Inter–Varsity Press, pg. 173.

4   From Immanuel, Rajappan D., *The Influence Of Hinduism On Indian Christians*, Jabalpur, 1950, pg. 11.

5   Goel, Sita Ram, *Catholic Ashrams: Adopting and Adapting Hindu Dharma*, Voice of India, New Delhi, 1988, pg. ix.

6   This is my summary from Dayanand Bharati, "A Review Article: Catholic Ashrams: Adopting and Adapting Hindu Dharma," in *To All Men All Things*, vol. 2 no. 2, August, 1992, pp. 4–6. The quotes from the book *Catholic Ashrams* are found on pages vi, xiii to xv, 4, 9.

7   Pushparaj, Dr., *Jamakkaran* [Tamil], June, 1992, pg. 17.

8   Robert Schmidt, op. cit. pg. 54.

9   In my recent talk with Rev. D. P. Titus at Sat Tal Ashram (September 18, 1998), he said that at Rewa when he was conducting *satsangh*, as some Operation Mobilization people came, he asked a Hindu convert to share. "But to my surprise and regret, that young man, though know Hindi very well, spoke only in English with another person to translate." What kind of impression would he have left on his audience, who were mostly Hindus?

10   Cf. G. U. Pope: "There exists now much of what is called Christian Tamil, a dialect created by the Danish missionaries of Tranquebar; enriched by generations of Tanjore, German, and other missionaries; modified, purified, and refrigerated by the Swiss Rhenuis and the very composite Tinnevelly school; expanded and harmonized by Englishmen, amongst whom Bower (a Eurasian) was foremost in his day; and, finally, waiting now for the touch of some heaven–born genius among the Tamil community to make it as sweet and effective as any language on earth, living or dead." (Op. cit. pg. xii.)

11   Lloyd–Jones, D. M., *Studies In The Sermon On The Mount* (Vol. II), Inter–Varsity Fellowship, London, 1966., pp. 192–93. In illustration, during my Himalayan visit in May 1990, I stayed with a *sanyasi* in his small cottage at Badrinath. That night (after midnight) I got an opportunity to share my faith in Christ. We talked for a long time till 3.00 a.m. and at the end he requested of me, "give me a copy of your 'Veda' through which you have attained *shanti* (peace, which in that context meant salvation)." And after my return, I sent him a New Testament.

12   Cf. Lipner: "*Bhagavan* has been variously explained, e.g. as 'the One who possesses and shares *bhaga* or bliss, well–being' or 'the One who possesses the six *bhagas* or attributes'." (Julius Lipner, *Hindus: Their Religious Beliefs and Practices*, Routledge, London, 1994, pp. 308–309) Cf. also Fallon: "In general, *Bhagavan* is not synonymous with any one name of the divine

manifestations or descents; it clearly designates the *Parama Purusa* or *Parama Atman*, the One 'personal' supreme deity. Words like *deva* (god) and *devi* (goddess), even words like *Isvara* (lord) or *devata* (deity) can be used in the plural number; *Bhagavan* is always singular....The *Bhagavata Purana* and other *bhakti* texts have developed still further this conception of the *Bhagavan*. But it transcends any particular sect or school, and the word *Bhagavan* has come to sum up within itself all that the Hindus feel and believe about God as personal Lord and Savior, independently of any particular reference to this or that Avatara." (P. Fallon, "God in Hinduism: Brahman, Paramatman, Isvara and Bhagavan," in de Smet and Neuner, (eds.), *Religious Hinduism*, Fourth Revised Edition, 1997, pp. 114–115.

13   Vedanayagam Sastriyar (1774–1864) is a fascinating study as this Tamil Christian poet was himself a convert who ridiculed several Hindu practices yet called God "Brahman, Saccitananda, Siva and Vishnu (Maal)" (Selva-nayagam, op. cit. pg.112–13) However this usage was in devotional writing of lyrics and not in theology as such.

14   Stott, John R., op. cit., pg. 173, 175.

15   Martin, Paul, *Missionary of the Indian Road: The Theology of Stanley Jones*, Theological Book Trust, Bangalore, 1996, pp. 83–84. Note further on this same point: "E. P. Rice and Edwin Greaves, both from the same mission-ary society as Farquhar, argued that Christ should be clearly distinguished from the Church in the missionary message....Greaves maintained that the antipathy towards Christianity as a Western religion could only be over-come by encouraging Indians to accept Christ, who was neither Western nor Eastern, without insisting on their joining a church" (pg. 82).

16   Quoted from Hesselgrave, David, *Today's Choices For Tomorrow's Mission*, pg. 153.

17   Op. cit. pg. 199.

18   Keller, Carl, "The Vedanta Philosophy and the Message of Christ," *International Review of Missions* 1956, pp. 377–389.

19   Hesselgrave, David, op. cit., pp. 160–1.

20   Datta, S. K., *The Desire of India*, London, l908, pp. 255f.

21   Andrews, C. F. *The Renaissance in India: Its Missionary Aspect*, London, 1912, pg. 289, quoted from Thomas, M. M., op. cit., pp. 278–9.

22   Ibid., pp. 278–9 (emphasis added).

23   Richard, H. L. (ed.), *R. C. Das: Evangelical Prophet for Contextual Christianity*, CISRS/ISPCK, Delhi, 1995, pg. 249. Those who oppose such an Indian voice (of Das) can listen Robert Schmidt:

Its greatest weakness is its present belief and practice that the training and payment of professional clergy is necessary for the churches' life and health....

Churches in the poor areas of the world are almost always dependent upon the Western churches for the theological education of native pastors/priests. In some cases this means sending young men abroad for training. In other instances, it means asking the richer West-ern churches for funds and manpower to erect and sustain theological schools. Since the churches in the poor nations cannot afford their own seminaries, Western churches continue to support and direct them, and, in effect, control the seminaries and formation of their graduates. (Op. cit. pp. 32–33)

24   Wald, S. N., "Christian Terminology in Hindi," in *Missionstudien* 1, 1962, pg. 231.

25   To my surprise, I find I am like the medieval monks, as I am listening to Indian classical [Carnatic] music, which the focus on Westernized Christian music deprived me of, at the cost of making me dry within.

26   Boyd, Robin, *Indian Christian Theology*, Madras, 1979, pp. 3–5.

27   Schmidt, op. cit. pg. 90.

28   Cf. Schmidt: "Greek thought differed greatly from Hebrew thought which preceded it. The Hebrew way of thinking was living and dynamic. Things progressed and regressed. Time moved on. In Hebrew, God thought and changed his mind. He repented and forgave....

Little of this is true in Greek thought. In it, neither God nor history move. Concepts tend to be static in nature. Greek thought, therefore, cannot abide contradiction. It is this or that, one or the other. Rarely do Greek categories permit a both/and. Seldom does one see dynamic growth and the flowering of one concept from another.

Not only is Greek thought fundamentally different from Hebrew thinking, it also contrasts with the modes of thought coming from Asia, African, and Native American cultures. In all of these cultures there is a much greater accommodation of seeming contradictions and a greater appreciation of growth and development. This is why missionaries almost universally report that people of these cultures find the Old Testament far closer to their cultures than doctrinal theology." (Ibid. pp. 89–90)

29   Hesselgrave, D., op. cit., pg. 151.

30   Boyd, op. cit., pg. 5. Cf. also Frank E Reynolds' comment on Francis Clooney's scholarly work *Theology after Vedanta*, wherein "one of the major achievements of Clooney's book is to show, beyond any doubt, that classical Advaita writings in general, and the work of Sankara in particular, are thoroughly theological." (from the foreword to Francis X. Clooney, *Theology after Vedanta: An Experiment in Comparative Theology*, Albany, State University of New York Press, 1993, pg. xiv.

31   Aleaz, K. P., *Christian Thought Through Advaita Vedanta*, ISPCK, Delhi, 1996, pg. 90 and pg. 2.

32   Ibid., pg. 99.

33   Clooney, S.J., op. cit. pp. 4–5.

34   Selvanayagam, op. cit., pg. 99.

35   For example for monism we can quote the famous *mahaavaakya* of *"aham brahmaasmi"* (I am Brahman) of Brhadaranyaka Upanishad 1.4.10; and for non–dualism (there are two but they are not two) *"tat tvam asi"* (You are that) of Chandogya Upanishad 6.8.7. But there is even some tension in such *mahaavaakyas*, as Clooney has pointed out: "A great saying such as "you are that" (*tat tvam asi*) upsets our reading of the Upanishads because, in the Advaita reading, it seems to equate two things that ought not to be equated: the phenomenal, finite self (*tvam*) and Brahman (*tat*)." (Op. cit. pg. 86)

36   *Age*, The Westminster Press, Philadelphia, 1984, pg. 69, quoted by Clooney, op. cit., pg. 231.

37 Wilkins, W. J., *Hindu Mythology: Vedic & Puranic*, 2nd edition, Heritage Publishers, New Delhi, 1991, pp. vii–viii.

38 Padinjarekara, Joseph, *Christ in Ancient Vedas*, Welch Publishing Company Inc, Burlington, Canada,1991, pg. 128.

39 From Hume, R. E., *The Thirteen Principal Upanishads*, Second Edition, Revised, Oxford University Press, Third impression 1985, Delhi, pg. 352.

40 This is clear in his books: *Fulfillment of the Vedic Quest in the Lord Jesus Christ* and in *St. John's Gospel: It's Witness to India*, and in the booklet *The Concept of Divine Sacrifice in the Bible and Vedic Scriptures*, all privately published by the author.

41 Titus, D.P. *St. John's Gospel: It's Witness to India*, pg. 88. Soma was an intoxicant used is some Vedic rituals that was made from a plant whose identity has never been definitively determined.

42 For an example of claims without references see the tract "Sacrifice" written by "the late Adhyaksha Anubhavananda Kesava Raya Sarma Mandapaka," often printed in English by the Gospel Literature Service (who should be ashamed of printing material without references) and in some other languages also. On false quotations note that Sadhu Chellappa in his tract "Lord, who art thou?" claims a quotation from Rig Veda 10.90, the Purusha sukta (*"Vishvakarma sarvani boothani juhavanch; kahasa aathmatha manthatho juhavancha kaha"*) which does not exist therein, and then gives a paraphrase which gives a completely imaginary meaning far removed from anything ever hinted at in any Hindu scripture: "Prajapathi who is called as Vishvakarma will sacrifice himself and shed his blood and redeem us." (See Swami Harshananda's *The Purusasukta: An Exegesis*, Bangalore, Ramakrishana Math, 1996, for textual analysis and translation of the Purusasukta.)

43 Richard, H. L., "The Arian Witness Recalled: Vedic Sacrifice and Fulfillment Theology," *To All Men All Things*, vol. 3 no. 3, Dec. 1993 and vol. 4 no. 1, Apr. 1994.

44 Boyd, R., op. cit., pg. 5.

45 This phrase is from a prayer offered at the worship service held on 12–10–1992 during the 23rd session of the Church of South India Synod at Palayamkottai.

46 As noted by Klostermaier, Klaus K., *Mythologies and Philosophies of Salvation in the Theistic Traditions of India*, Ontario, Wilfred Laurier University Press, 1984 pg. 134. The entire section on "Basic Mythology Concerning Siva as Savior" [pp. 126–159] is worthy of study.

47 Lloyd–Jones, D. M., op. cit. pp.185–86.

48 For an illustration of Hindu misuse of the Bible note this from Swami Vivekananda:

> The Christian believes that God took the shape of a dove, and came down, and they think this is history, and not mythology. But the Hindu believes that god is manifested in the cow. Christians say that is mythology, and not history: superstition....Nobody in the world as far as I have seen is able to find out the fine distinction between history and mythology in the brains of these gentlemen. All those stories are mythological, mixed up with a little history.

(Quoted from V. Rangarajan, "Vedanta Embraces Christianity," in *Christianity in India: A Critical Study*, op. cit., pg. 198.)

There are plenty of such incidents we could study. Note these objections to Swami Vivekananda's statements: firstly, it was not God the Father but the Holy Spirit who came in the shape of a dove, in a clearly defined historical situation. Secondly, the Holy Spirit descended to reveal Jesus Christ to John the Baptist specifically as he was baptizing many people. This was clearly a temporary and one—time event, not the actual and permanent coming of God in the form of a dove. Thirdly, nowhere in Christendom, not even among Roman Catholics (who keep a lot of images) is the form of a dove kept to worship as the Hindus do at times with the cow or monkey. The Holy Spirit came on Jesus to reveal who Jesus was to John the Baptist. It was a sign for him as he was the forerunner of the Messiah.

49   Panikkar, R., *A Dwelling Place for Wisdom*, New Delhi, Motilal Banarsidass, 1995, pp.115–118.

50   Selvanayagam, op. cit., pg.115.

51   Ibid., pg. 114.

52   The words quoted are from Fr. Ishwar Prasad in *Christian Ashrams: A Movement with a Future?* Vandana Mataji, ed., ISPCK, Delhi, 1993, pg.105.

53   Time and again I hear that as Jesus was buried and resurrected, we too must follow His example. But even missionaries like E. Stanley Jones have been cremated, and nowadays in England some 90% of Christians burn their dead because space is not available to bury them. The Christian graveyard has become a stumbling block rather than an aid for Hindus to understand the resurrection world–view. While coming from Varanasi by train to Lucknow, one can see a big Christian graveyard. Once when I was traveling, a Hindu commented that "Hinduism is the best religion. See, the Christians even after death don't want to leave this world and their desire for possession remains. Even after death they occupy more than six feet of land, which could be used for housing purpose considering the demand. As their religion is promising only a heaven with gold and diamonds, they still want to hold on to this world. Whereas Hinduism promises *mukti*; it releases us from the vanity of this world. That is why we burn the dead and do not waste the land."

54   If two witnesses are desired to demonstrate the point, consider this story from my best friend and co–worker Paul Kannan of Erode: During one of his children's classes in a Bible study at Salem, he asked a boy where he is studying. The boy said "The school next to the *paye koil* (devil's temple)." Confused with such an answer, Kannan specifically asked the name of the school. The boy said it, and Kannan recognized both the school as well the temple. But startled by such a response from the boy, he asked, "Who said that it is a *paye koil*. "Daddy" was the boy's response. Later Kannan challenged that man to think: "Being a convert yourself, if you teach your children in such a way, what will your neighbors and relatives think about you? How are you going to share your faith with your own people while entertaining such an attitude towards their deities and temple, which you have also worshipped? Respect the other's faith, no matter how you may disagree with them." Of course, Kannan understood that man's plight because he also had been taught this way by the Christians in his church.

55   Those who are interested in reading a scholarly discussion of Hindu cultural marks (particularly that of women) may see: "Tilaka Mark," by Professor P. V. Kane, in S.G. Moghe (ed), *Professor Kane's Contribution to Dharmasastra Literature*, D.K. Printworld, New Delhi, 1997, pp. 233–37.

56   "I am ever present in all living beings as their very Self (Inner Controller). A man (therefore) who worships Me through an idol, showing disrespect to Me (as abiding in all creatures), makes a travesty of worship, Ignoring me, the Supreme Ruler, the Self present in all living beings, he who stupidly resorts to idol–worship alone throws oblations into the ashes" (3.29.21–22; from Goswami, C. L., *Srimad Bhagavata Mahapurana*, Gita Press, Gorakhpur, 2nd ed., 1982, vol. 1, pg. 301)

57   See the suggestive comments of R. C. Das in this direction in Richard, H. L., op. cit., pg. 131. Note that biblical denunciations of idol worship are addressed to the Jews, who should have known better, not to people outside the covenant God made with Israel. Note also how respectfully Paul addressed the idolaters in Athens (Acts 17).

58   For further comments on this point see my article "The Menace of Full Time Ministry," *To All Men All Things*, vol. 4, no. 3, Dec. 1994. Regarding the relevancy of tentmakers (in every context) Robert Schmidt says:

Locally educated "bi–vocational pastors" are also doing an excellent job in ethnic communities in the United States and elsewhere. These are people who work both in the secular world to earn an income and also work in the church as opportunities present themselves. Here the advantages of educating people from a given ethnic group who know the language, customs and traditions of their people is readily apparent. Not only are such pastors able to relate the Gospel to the culture of their people, they also have the credibility that comes from sharing in the work–a–day job experiences of their people. (Op. cit. pg. 29)

Above all, "Professionally trained and paid leaders too often are separate from the culture of their congregations by virtue of their professional education and training," says Schmidt. He explains this point further: "Countless pastors and priests can testify to the truth of this observation. Too often lay people do not come to the clergy for help because they do not believe that clergy persons can understand their lives and their problems." (Ibid. pg. 31)

59   Janaki, a Brahmin girl and *bhakta* of Jesus, after her marriage went to the temple when her husband asked her to go. But her mother and house owner, who know of her faith in Christ, later asked "to whom did you pray in the temple?" "Jesus," replied Janaki. And her conviction is that she obeyed her husband when he asked her to go to the temple, and she would not hide her faith when asked particularly. To such a person our answer should be "go in peace."

60   The very word "son" (*putra*) is rooted in this concept, as O'Flaherty points out: "The son is said to save (*tra*) his father from the hell called Put (by offering the oblation to the ancestors), and hence a son is called *putrá*." (Wendy Doniger O'Flaherty, *The Origins of Evil in Hindu Mythology*, University of California Press, Los Angeles, 1976, pg. 325) A disciple of Christ may not believe in this, but he cannot remove it entirely from the minds of his relatives, although how many of them truly believe it is an open question.

61   Roland Allen, *The Spontaneous Expansion of the Church and the Causes which Hinder It*, WS Publishers, 1997, pg. 48.

62   "In order to 'Egyptianize' Joseph, Pharaoh gave him an Egyptian name
      and an Egyptian wife. The meaning of his Egyptian name is uncertain.
      Asenath means 'she belongs to Neith' (a goddess of the Egyptians)." Ryrie,
      C. Caldwell, *Ryrie Study Bible*, Moody Press, Chicago, 1978, pg. 74.

63   Olson, op. cit., pg. 168.

64   Ibid., pg. 169. Cf. also this insight from the Old Testament from Wright:
      "Man, his image, was created to live in the harmony of personal equality
      but with social organization that required functional structures of author-
      ity. The ordering of social relationships and structures, locally, nationally
      and globally, is of direct concern to our Creator God, then." (Christopher
      J. H. Wright, op. cit. pg. 105) And this is well illustrated from life of Rev.
      Kalicaran Banerjea:

      No one in the family disregarded him because he was a Christian; rather, when formal respect
      was to be shown this fact would be ignored. Kalicaran laid to rest the view that by becoming
      a Christian one separates from one's Hindu kin so decisively that later the missionaries found
      it very easy to make Christians. He would observe the customs of Bhai—phota and jamai—sas-
      thi; during Sarasvati Puja he would do worship to his books; he regarded his mother as a de-
      ity. (Barber, B.R., *Kali Charan Banurji: Brahmin, Christian, Saint.* The Christian Literature
      Society for India, London, Madras and Colombo, 1912, pg. 39)

65   Rangarajan, V., op. cit. pp. 192–193, emphasis mine.

66   Cf. Wright: "The Bible…makes no unnatural separation between 'politics'
      and 'religion,' though neither does it identify them. Both are essential
      dimensions of what it is to be human. Man the worshipper is also man the
      political animal, for God made him so." (Christopher J.H. Wright, op. cit.
      pg. 105)

67   The church building is not a place where God lives, but a meeting hall
      where Christians gather. Cf. Selvanayagam's observation that "It is very
      significant to note that in the area of religious structures, beliefs and prac-
      tices, Hindus are more truthful to their original traditions and scriptures.
      But Christian Indians have fallen into the complex trap of uncritical and
      unconscious indigenization. Consequently…. the Church building, the
      meeting place of the congregation for worship and service, is called a
      temple…" (op. cit. pg. 143)

68   About this tradition Schmidt says:

      A careful look at the early history of the church shows that church buildings began at approxi-
      mately the same time as did the growth of a full–time, resident, professional clergy….

      By this time church buildings have become such a recognized part of the Christian Church
      that it is almost impossible for us to conceive of the Christian Church without them. Yet for
      several centuries the church got along without them very easily. What a difference between
      that era and our own!…

      The wealth that congregations have stuffed into buildings has greatly impoverished the
      churches of the West. (Op. cit. pg. 35)

69   Ansar Hussain Khan, *The Rediscovery of India A New Subcontinent*, Orient
      Longman Limited 1995, Hyderabad, 1995, pg. 102.

70   Alexander, E. S., *The Attitudes of British Protestant Missionaries Towards
      Nationalism in India with Special Reference to Madras Presidency, 1919–
      1927*, Konark Publishers, New Delhi, 1994, pg. 103.

71 Yesudasan, Savarirayan, *Daivabhaktiyam Desabhaktiyam*, (Tamil), Tiru-pathur, 1940 [1931], pg. 6.

72 Op. cit. pg. 132.

73 Cf. Shashi Tharoor: "*Divide et impera*, they called it in the language of their own Roman conquerors – divide and rule….As soon as the national revolt…."Sepoy Mutiny" – was put down, British officials rediscovered their Latin lessons. *Divide et impera* was the subject of closely argued policy–minutes; everything had to be done to drive wedges between Indi-ans in the interests of the whites and Whitehall. The British did not have far to look to place their wedges: they found the perfect opportunities in the religious distinctions which India, in its tolerance, had so long and so innocently preserved." (*The Great Indian Novel*, Picador, 1994, pg. 141)

74 To know further about the British mistakes, it is recommended to read Shashi Tharoor's *The Great Indian Novel*, Picador, 1994, written as fiction but full of fact; also Ansar Hussain Khan, *The Rediscovery of India :A New Subcontinent*, Orient Longman Limited 1995, Hyderabad, (A.P.) India, 1995 and Raychaudhuri, Tapan, *Perceptions, Emotions, Sensibilities: Essays on India's Colonial and Post–Colonial Experiences*, Oxford University Press, New Delhi, 1999.

75 Mangalwadi, Vishal, *India: The Grand Experiment*, Pippa Rann Books, Surrey, 1997. Note the bitter review of this book by R. Prasannan in *The Week*, Vol. 15 No. 35, Aug. 17, 1997; a review which certainly reflects a great deal of Hindu opinion on such writings and which shows such books doing more harm than good in communication to Hindus.

76 Savarirayan, op. cit. pg. 30.

77 Khan, op. cit., pg. 208.

78 Vempeny, Ishanand, *Krsna And Christ*, Gujarat Sahitya Prakash, Anand, 1988, pg. 436.

79 Lipner 1999, op. cit pg. 38.

80 In Richard, H. L., op. cit., pg. 189.

CHAPTER FOUR

CHRIST'S BHAKTAS IN
MODERN INDIA

A blanket rejection of all that this book represents is not an unfamiliar statement: "India is rapidly becoming a secular country due to scientific development (already ours is a secular country by constitution). Hindus are fast losing their faith in their religion and their social structure is also quickly collapsing. They are becoming more materialistic. Educated, city dwelling people are no more under the spell of blind faith. Even village people—thanks to the mass media like television with Music and Star TV channels—are developing fast. Moreover, because they are losing their religious system (to some extent culturally and socially also), they are open to any and every change. Whereas, you want us to go back to 10th and 5th centuries A. D. and even B. C. in the name of contextualization."

It is true that India (as the entire world) is in a time of rapid transition. Every change in a society will bring initial confusion and shock. In spite of this, a well organized society will soon recover from it and prove its capacity to receive any positive changes without compromising its structure and cultural heritage. This has been proven so far in India. In spite of several shocks and changes that she faced, she remains intact till this day. Whatever may be the scientific and materialistic influence, after a period of chaos and confusion and paying an initial cost for it, she will return back to her originality. All Hindus may become modern and they may even give up their blind religious faith; their caste and social systems may undergo a radical change, but there are only two options left before them—either they will lose their very identity as Indian and thoroughly disintegrate, or they will emerge as a more powerful, refined nation after paying a severe price for too much materialism and modernism. The hopes are for the latter not the former.

A point of caution should also be made here. Nowadays there is a call being given by Hindu "fundamentalists" (a slippery term) to bring India back to its past glory. It is true that "Hindu revivalists use religion as a cover for political ends" and also that

> political leaders.... therefore both seek to support the Hindu cause while at the same time harping on secular values. The present policy of politicizing religion and communalizing politics can be attributed to lack of genuine commitment to either religion or secularism. Each religion in India needs to contribute its distinctive values towards the emergence of a secular society and a global ethic.[1]

While agreeing with this, we must also see the other side of the coin. In the name of opposing religious fundamentalism, the so–called guardians of secularism create communalism (here I mean caste–based communalism among the Hindus, as seen in recent caste riots in South Tamil Nadu) to achieve their political ends and that is why Hindu fundamentalists condemn the communal secularist as a pseudo–secularist. While both extreme groups blame each other, we poor common people are caught between a rock and a hard place. In this situation, the so–called spiritual people say that they will have nothing to do with such a political struggle because they just want to live peacefully in their religious tranquility. Particularly within the Christian community, it seems to be considered anathema even to think and talk on such issues. But, as Leslie Newbigin points out, "One can almost say that the central strand of the Old Testament story is the struggle of the prophet to speak the word of the living God in relation to the secular events of his time, and against the religion of his time." [2] Therefore, if we keep away from such involvement in national events, we are actually helping the dark forces of fundamentalism and communalism to control us.

One thing is sure: that we cannot blame the Hindus and their social structure for all the problems that are threatening India in the name of modernism and materialism. At the same time, we cannot deny that "Christianity" has to some extent contributed to this rise of materialism and modernism, for good or evil. And Westernized Christianity is certainly not the remedy for these problems in India. I was very surprised and even shocked by one mature Christian leader with vast experience, when in sharing his strategy paper, he suggested that because modernism and materialism are shaking the very foundation of Hinduism, this is the best opportunity to win many Hindus to Christianity. If we think that the changes that materialism and modernism are bringing to India are a blessing in disguise because they will help us to win them easily for Christianity, then we are merely trying to fish in troubled water. Modernism and materialism are more a threat to Westernized Christian society than to the Hindus.

The resurgence of Hinduism is stronger than ever before. Whenever I meet any *bhakta* of Christ from an upper caste, I share my views on indigenization and the need to be deeply Indian while following Christ. Generally I find a quick and encouraging response from them. One such person is Mohan Kumar. After my talk with him for just an hour, and his reading of *Jesus Christ and the Hindu Community* by Hans Staffner and a few other articles, he suddenly realized the greatness of our cultural heritage and wrote to me, "Please, we would appreciate it if could let us know a few other books you could recommend to *fuel our burning desire to know more about our great country*."

If this is the case with a *bhakta* of Christ in whom we can raise the spirit of "Remain Indian while following Christ," how much more the RSS, BJP and VHP can provoke the staunch Hindus. The educated Hindus see the value of their social and cultural heritage as the correct remedy and antidote for extreme modernism. A strong revival is again coming after the Renaissance movements. Though secularization and modernization

due to scientific developments "de–mythologized" Hinduism,
it also led to the revival, the return back to their past heritage
which so far has kept them intact.[3] Nowadays not only the
so–called upper castes, but even many of the educated so–called
backward people are not ready to follow "Christianity" because
in it, they see a threat to their very identity as Indians.

In all of this, we request Indian Christians not to do anything new or unbiblical. We simply ask them to go back to the
New Testament ways of reaching people, removing their European ways. At the same time, we need not imitate exactly what
Paul has done. We can take the principles and apply them to our
own situation rather than blindly imposing Western traditions
in our approach to reach people for Christ.

The one statement that seems to most shock as well as
disturb Christians during my teaching and sharing is that *I am
a Hindu and a bhakta of Christ but not a Christian*. Whatever
reasons and explanations I give about the term "Hindu" do not
seem to convince them. (I have discussed this at length in the
forthcoming book *Understanding Hinduism*.) Their only argument is based on the word "Christian" in Acts 11:26. Again and
again, they will say that those who follow Christ are Christians.
Therefore, if you are a follower of Christ, then naturally and
automatically you become a Christian, and can no more remain
a Hindu. Even one person vehemently argued, "You may say
that you are a Hindu and follower of Jesus Christ, but others see you only as a Christian." Who is to be blamed for this?
Christianity in India created such a mental atmosphere among
the Hindus that one cannot remain culturally and socially as a
Hindu and follow Jesus Christ, but rather he must automatically
give up everything Hindu and become "Christian." However, in
their argument they forget one fact; that is that they lack proper
support for their stand for the word "Christian" from the Bible.
What they say and even impose is their own tradition, as usual
inherited by (or imposed on) them from others. Interestingly,
present followers of Christ from among the Jews are calling
themselves "Messianic Jews" and not "Christians," and this is

easily accepted in the Christian world. Still many expect Hindu followers of Christ to become "Christian."

We must remember that every practice—both Scriptural and non–scriptural—started somewhere only on a small level, and it took several hundred years to grow into a popular, unchallenge-able, unquestionable position, leaving a permanent impression in the hearts and minds of people. Moreover, when some new ideas arise challenging such a long existing tradition, they not only disturb those who profess it, but face a lot of opposition from them. The main reason for such opposition is the lack of proper understanding about the tradition, which is rather blindly fol-lowed, mainly as they see some kind of threat to their mental security which is at stake due to the new ideas. The best example is the persecution of the scientist by the church in the Middle Ages. Anyway, we cannot refrain from sharing what we believe just to make others feel comfortable. Therefore, those who want to tread any new path must be prepared to pay a heavy cost for their conviction.

Now the first important point to notice on the term "Hindu" is that an academic explanation of this word does not occur in any of the Hindu scriptures. The word "Hindu," coming from "Sindu" River, originally held geographical rather than religious meaning, which later become "India" and "Hindu," as Hans Staffner summarizes,

> It appears that in none of the scriptural and semi–scriptural books is the term "Hindu" used to describe a particular religion. In the Sanskrit lan-guage the term "Hindu" does not seem to occur at all. Neither do the *Ve-das*, the *Upanishads,* the *Bhagavad–Gita,* the *Smritis* nor the *Puranas* ever talk of a Hindu religion. The *bhakti* poets speak of a *Bhagavata dharma,* but never of a *Hindu dharma.* To describe different religions appropriate terms were used: *Saiva, Vaishnava, Jaina,* etc. It is doubtful whether before the colonial era anyone ever spoke of a "HINDU RELIGION."[4]

The Europeans, who are always interested in new inventions in every field, were also the pioneers to "invent" the religion called Hinduism. Because they are also famous for "imposing" their own ideas on others, they gradually brainwashed Indians and others to believe that all those non–Christians, non–Mus-lims, etc., are confessing a religion called "Hinduism." As Hein-

rich von Stietencron, Professor of Indology and Comparative
Religion at the University of Tubingen, writes:

> The word "Hinduism" is not a term which any religion in India applies
> to itself, but is something which Europeans have invented. This word
> was meant to designate the religion of the Hindus. Unfortunately the
> people who invented this concept did not know enough about the
> Hindus. They discovered too late that the Hindus have many religions.
> Hinduism is considered as one of the great world religions. Today we
> realize, though we find it difficult to admit, that *the Hindu religion is
> a plant, which has artificially been cultivated by European scholars*–a
> plant, which is much too beautiful to be thrown away; still, *it is an arti-
> ficial plant; in nature it does not exist.*[5]

Of course this is an academic or even an "artificial" answer.
Even though it gives the "real" information, yet it is too book-
ish. In the popular context, though a Hindu is a member of a
particular community or society irrespective of his faith, yet it
also is now used to designate those who profess the "religion"
called "Hinduism." Hence in reality, this "artificial plant" does
now exist and is carefully nurtured by the Hindu fundamentalists who wish to "make India Hindu." [6] "Hinduism" also popu-
larly exists in the minds of Christians, who with much allergy
and pain (perhaps even with a kind of hidden hatred) approach
the artificial plant to pluck a few fruits (viz., Hindus, in most
cases picked up from those which have already fallen down
due to being properly ripened by the grace of God, or in some
cases having fallen due to heavy wind before being ripened) to
fill their "Christian baskets" to be sent to their own respective
denominational markets.

The term "Christian" has a complicated a history. "Those
who follow Christ are the Christians" is the general definition
given by evangelical Christians. For this they will quote Acts 11:
26. They want to suggest that there exist no "nominal," "traditional," "denominational," etc., varieties of "Christians," these
all being counterfeits. Nevertheless, everybody knows that this is
also an artificial definition. Even in their evangelism work, they
will, with much pain and disturbance, explain the difference
between "nominal Christian" and "TRUE Christian" and will
waste 90% of their time and energy in giving such definitions

and descriptions for nominal and born again "Christians" which
forced me to write the following lines:

CHRIST–in or CHRISTIANS

Born again Christian
Brainwashed   "
Compound   "
Convention   "
Christmas   "
Care–free   "
Converted   "
Convicted   "
Dogmatic   "
Denominational "
By birth   "
Marriage   "
Nominal   "
New   "
Revived   "
Rice   "
Traditional   "
True   "
R. C.   "
Orthodox   "
Protestant   "
Pentecostal   "

O Lord! In this
World of Christians
Could you find one
True Christian
Who can claim
to be a Real Christ–in!?

In reality, especially to an average Hindu but also even to
most "Christians," a Christian is one who professes the religion
called "Christianity" founded by Jesus Christ. They have two
groups (even *jatis*; note the same word used by Dr. Yesudasan
in his book which is quoted above) called Roman Catholic and
Protestant, fighting with each other to dismiss the other as not
really Christian. Many never know that only "born again believers" are "TRUE Christians," etc. A bigger problem, especially for
evangelicals, is that the definition of "Christian" as "the follow-

ers of Christ" is only a definition based on tradition and is not
Biblical, however valuable that definition may be. A number of
points can be made to demonstrate this fact.

Firstly, the word "Christian" is not used by the apostles or
by the believers of the early church as we use it today. Take it
for granted that the believers at Antioch were called for the first
time as Christians, yet the term was neither accepted nor used
by the apostles except in Acts 11:26 and 26:28 and in I Peter 4:
16. In all these places the meaning is not in the sense that we
use today, as we shall show later. Leaving the other apostles, the
Apostle John, who lived long and was the last one in the apostolic circles to die, who had seen the growth, persecution and
rise of a few heresies in the early church, never used the word
"Christian" in any of his extant writings.

Secondly, the word "Christian" used at Antioch was not a
word of commendation. It never meant that those believers at
Antioch lived a glorious, spiritual, Christ–like life, on seeing
which others with much reverence and respect called them as
"Christians." They used the word to identify the believers, perhaps even to mock them (as Westerners were called *Paranghis,*
Brahmins are called *Paapan* and Muslims as *Tulukkan* in Tamil
in place of the respectful terms.)

However, let us grant that people at Antioch after seeing the
witnessing, spiritual life of the believers were very much im-
pressed and called them as "Christians" in the sense of "strict
followers of their Lord Jesus Christ." In a similar way, if Hindus
and other non–Christians, after seeing a Spirit filled, Christ–like
life in us, call us "Christians" then we can happily identify ourselves with Christians. Still, we all know the popular meaning
of the word "Christian" as interpreted by Hindus (and even by
Christians) so then why should we also accept that demeaning
word for our position in Christ?

Now let us see what some of the commentaries say about
the word "Christian" in each of the three occurrences in the
New Testament. First, Acts 11:26. I. Howard Marshall offers
this explanation:

One important result of all this activity was that for the first time the disciples became known as "Christians." Luke specially mentions this because "Christian" had become a familiar term in certain areas at the time when he wrote. Early in the second century the name is attested for Rome, Asia Minor and Antioch, and nothing prevents the view that it first came into use at Antioch. The ending of the word (Christians) indicates that it is a Latin word, like "Herodian" and that it refers to the followers of Christ. "Christ" will then be understood as a proper name, although its original use was as a title, "the Messiah," for Jesus. The verb, "were called," implies in all probability that "Christians" was a nickname given by the populace of Antioch, and thus "Christ" could well have been understood as a proper name by them, even if at this stage the Christians themselves still used it as a title; it was not long, however, before the title became increasingly more like a name for Jesus. It is likely that the name contained an element of ridicule (cf. Acts 26:28; I Pet. 4:16, its only other New Testament uses). *The Christians preferred to use other names for themselves, such as "disciples," "saints" and "brothers."* [7]

F. F. Bruce gives further insight:

Lit. "they did business (Gk. *chrematizo*) under the name of Christian," i.e. became commonly known by this name. Only from Gentiles could they have received this name (meaning "Christ's people") for "Christ" was a mere personal name in Gentile ears, whereas to Jews it meant "Messiah's people." [8]

Now on Acts 26:28, again from Marshall:

Agrippa realized what he would be letting himself in for if he gave an affirmative answer to Paul's question. If he confessed belief in the prophets, the obvious follow—up would be, "Surely then you accept that Jesus is the Messiah?" On the other hand, to deny that he believed in the prophets would be unthinkable for a loyal Jew. So he answers: "In a short time you think to make me a Christian!" The reply is light—hearted, but not ironic. It is Agrippa's attempt to get out of the logical trap in which he is in danger of being caught. [9]

Bruce's comment:

So he says, "In short, you are trying to persuade me to play the Christian" — for that is the true sense of his words. [10]

Finally, 1 Peter. 4:16. David Wheaton comments:

"Christian" occurs on only two other occasions in the New Testament, in Acts 11:26 and 26:28. In both cases, it is generally assumed to have been used by others as a term of contempt, but there are two other possible derivations, which may have significance. The Latin suffix *ianus* may have been added to the Greek word Christ to indicate "supporters of," in the same way that Herod's followers were called *"Herodians"* (Mk. 3:6, etc.) On the other hand, a Roman custom followed in adoption was that the person adopted into a Roman family took their name with this suffix and used it as his own. A person adopted into the family of Domitius would call himself Domitianus, and as Antioch was a very Roman city, the Christians there may well have applied the name to themselves as having been adopted into Christ's family."

Of course no amount of argument is going to bring an immediate solution to our problem. Because even our own people (I mean Hindus) after hearing of our conviction about Jesus Christ, even when we say that, "We are only *Yesu bhaktas* and not Christians," are not ready to buy our theory. They themselves clearly understand that confessing Christ means one "becomes" a Christian, i.e. changes his religious community whether he is a believer or not or holds church membership or not.

This can be understood from the following incident. In Bangalore, a convert Hindu couple from so–called high caste background initially called themselves as Hindu Christ *bhaktas*. But then they "officially declared" themselves as "Christians" and this greatly disturbed the man's parents. His father said to me, "My family came to an end with myself." For him, for a Hindu to "become" a "Christian" is not a change of heart but a change of community, and even marks an end to his family. The man's said to me, "So far my son said that he is a Hindu and *bhakta* of Christ. You too are a Hindu, and I know that you are a *bhakta* of Christ. I know from your life and talk that we can remain Hindu and be *bhaktas* of Christ. So why did my son and his wife change their minds now? Why can you not stop it?" She shed tears while sharing this. She had opened her heart for the Lord, but this move of her son brought a jolt to her mind, and she was deeply affected emotionally. In my answer, I said that the decision their son took was personal and was not based on my principles. When the couple tried to justify their change to me ("We were baptized, married and now have become members in the church, so we are Christians."), I pointed out to them that their change may help to increase the membership of their church, but it will not help their family members to follow the Lord.

Ours is a *struggle for existence*. As we have pointed out, every system started somewhere only on a small level and it took several hundred years to get recognition. Similarly, our claim as *"Yesu bhaktas* and still Hindus" may take several hundred years to get proper recognition both in India and elsewhere. Unlike others, we have to struggle on both ends—with Christians on one side and Hindus on the other. Now this struggle becomes yet more complicated because of the fight between the "fundamentalists" and "pseudo–secularists" to achieve their political ends.

Nevertheless, conviction is not a small affair and one has to count the cost that must be paid for it. Those who want to see the coming of the *kingdom of God* (not Christianity as it is understood and interpreted by everyone) among the so–called high caste people in India must accept these challenges with which we have wrestled in the pages of this book. As a result, learning from their own experiences, all the Christ *bhaktas* in India should persevere with much patience, and accepting all the criticisms from every corner, must be prepared to pay the cost for following Jesus *as Hindus.*

TATASTU! SHANTI!

Notes

1   Selvanayagam, op. cit., pg. 61.

2   Newbigin, L., *Honest Religion for Secular Man*, Lucknow Publishing House, Lucknow, 1966, pg. 95.

3   Mentioning "past heritage" does not mean one has succumbed to the artificial "Golden Age theory" invented by some Western scholars and promoted by the Indian Nationalists in their struggle against British rule in the 19th and 20th centuries. Note these perceptive comments on that theme:

> ... the tension between cultural preservation and modernization was solved through the invention of a distant Golden Age which was both indigenous and in accord with modern values. The idea of the Golden age was to become one of the cornerstones of Hindu nationalism....Dealing with ethnic nationalism, Smith analyzes the impact of European modernity on the wider world as having caused a sense of backwardness and decline among colonized and dominated peoples, from which a certain elite stratum, chiefly comprising the intelligentsia, then set about reforming their traditions. Subsequently, their main concern was to endow that renewed tradition with the sanction of a theoretical "Golden Age," an ideological reinterpretation of the past, perfectly fashioned in order to meet the challenge of the West. This historicist construction is the cornerstone of nationalism since it allows peoples threatened by European modernity to regain their self–respect by appropriating the strong points of the aggressor (Christophe Jaffrelot, *The Hindu Nationalist Movement and Indian Politics 1925 to the 1990s*, Penguin Books, 1999 (1993), pg. 11, 13)

And regarding its origin and Orientalists' contribution Rambachan says:

> The conception of the Golden Age directly influenced the reformist arguments of men like Rammohun Roy and was perhaps the early Orientalists' greatest contribution: "Knowledge of this golden age would become the cohesive ideology underlying a new sense of community. It is doubtful that the rise of nationalism would have been possible without the sense of community, the sense of community without a collective feeling of self–respect, and self–respect without the stimulus of a rediscovered golden age." (Rambachan, op. cit. pg. 14, quoting David Kopf, *British Orientalism and the Bengal Renaissance,* Berkeley: University of California Press, 1969, pg. 284)

4   Staffner, H., op. cit., pg. 91.

5   Quoted from Staffner, ibid., pg. 95, from *Christentum und Weltreligionen*, H. Kung (ed), Piper, Munich, 1984, p. 213–219 (emphasis added). Note this further elaboration from Stietencron:

> The very term "Hindu," from which "Hinduism" is derived and which was taken over by Western administrators, scholars and merchants from the Persian, caused misunderstandings in the West. The word is the Persian variant of Sanskrit *sindhu*, the Indus River, a word applied already in the Avesta both to the river and to the country through which the Indus flows. In the plural, it denotes the population living in that region: the Indus people, the Indians. This meaning is attested in Old Persian cuneiform inscriptions from the time of Darius I who expanded his realm to the Indus in 517 B. C. For more than 1000 years, the word Hindu (plural) continued to denote the Indians in general. But when, from 712 A. D. onwards, Muslims began to settle permanently in the Indus valley and to make converts among low–caste Hindus, Persian authors distinguished between Hindus and Muslims in India: Hindus were Indians other than Muslim. We know that Persian scholars were able to distinguish a number of religions among the Hindus. But when Europeans started to use the term Hindoo, they applied it to the non–Muslim masses of India without those scholarly differentiations. Most people failed to realize that the term "Hindu" corresponded exactly to their own word "Indian" which is derived, like the name "India," from the same Indus River, the *indos* of the Greek. The Hindu, they knew, was distinct from the Muslims, the Jew, the Christian, the Parsee and the Jain who were all present in the Indian coastal area known to Western trade. Therefore, they took the term "Hindu" to designate the follower of a particular Indian religion. This was a fundamental

misunderstanding of the term. And from the Hindu the term "Hinduism" was derived by way of abstraction, denoting an imagined religion of the vast majority of the population — something that had never existed as a "religion" (in the Western sense) in the consciousness of the Indian people themselves. ("Hinduism: On the Proper Use of a Deceptive Term" in *Hinduism Reconsidered*, edited by Sontheimer, Gunther D. and Kulke, Hermann, Manohar Books, Delhi, 1991, pp. 11–12.

6   Cf. David Ludden's insightful comments on this line: "The practices of labeling things Indian with the term "Hindu" has caused endless confusion, obliterating lines between religious and census classifications....This phrasing reinforces in the mind of the reader the idea that Hinduism constitutes India in a way that really is untrue; however, because the government of India is not Hindu, "predominantly" or otherwise; it is less so, in fact, than the United States government is Christian, because most political parties in India explicitly oppose Hindu politics. The effect of this phrasing is to identify India, the Indian people, and the Indian government as being Hindu by definition. Making this identification into a political reality is in fact the project of Hindu nationalism. (As I write, the *New York Times*, July 10, 1995, describes India as "predominantly Hindu" in its report explaining India's conflict with Pakistan over Kashmir, a usage that implicitly endorses Hindu nationalism.)" (op. cit. pp. 7–8)

7   *The Acts of the Apostles*, Tyndale New Testament Commentaries, IVP, London, 1983, pg. 203, emphasis added.

8   In Guthrie, D. and Motyer, J. A. (eds.), *New Bible Commentary*, Inter–Varsity Press, third edition, Leicester, 1978, pg. 987.

9   Marshall, I. H., op. cit. pp. 399–400.

10   Bruce, F. F., op. cit. pg. 1007.

11   Wheaton, David, H. , in Guthrie, D, etc. *New Bible Commentary* op. cit. pg. 1246.

APPENDIX A

ON THE PROPRIETY OF
CHRISTIAN WOMEN WEARING
THE RED DOT

by P. Chenchiah

(From The Guardian, 1951, pg. 429, reprinted in Thangasamy, D. A. (ed.), The Theology of Chenchiah, YMCA/CISRS, 1966, pp. 233–4.)

Sir—The red–dot controversy, started in the columns of your esteemed journal and illumined by illustrious contributors, reveals attitudes which are creditable neither to our intellect nor to our spirituality.

The simple truth of the matter is that the red–dot comes from the vanity box of women—which is as old as Eve. To stray into theological and anthropological discussion about it is simply ridiculous. It is just a fashion and a fashion has no reason or logic about it.

The association of the red–dot with the phallic symbol is less scientific than the association of the lip–stick and powder–box with primitive Druid ritual and worship. If you begin to trace things to their remote origins you will find that there is hardly anything in our dress, jewels and food, which has not sprung from paganism and heathenism. The under–done meal, which rejoices many a Western stomach and heart, and the tango dance are direct descendants of African customs. Would the champions of anti–red–dot campaign lead a war against the lip–stick, the powder–box, the tango and the under–done meal?

One point more; it is not the red–dot only that has heathen associations. More palpably and less dubiously it can be shown that Christian altars, priests' vestments, churches [Gothic], sacraments, and festivals, have heathen ancestry. Why shy at the red–dot only? Of all things, I hate with my Lord the Pharisaism that strains at the gnat and swallows the camel.

APPENDIX B

ON THE USE OF OM

by Christ Bhaktas

After research and collecting information from various sources, based on my knowledge as a layman the following are my opinions regarding using the word *om* in Christian worship.

1   *Om* is just an impersonal word, whatever may be the later developments in giving some meaning to it. It is like *Sri,* which is being used to some gods like Sri Rama, etc. So we cannot address it or pray to it or even meditate on it. Can we meditate on the word *Sri*?

2   By using *om* for Jesus as John used *logos,* we cannot add any new theological insight to Christology that would be relevant to Indian contexts. John was inspired by the Holy Spirit to use *logos* in Scripture; whereas, we cannot claim such apostolic authority to add any new meaning to Jesus Christ, even though it would be relevant to our context in India.

3   Using cultural symbols and religious symbols are different matters. Though in some areas in India both culture and religion are intermingled, yet *om* is purely a religious symbol. Therefore, we must exercise care in our use of it. Also, I have some personal reservation in using the sym-

bol of *om* either in picture or metal in Christian ashrams. For example, in Jeevanjyothi Ashram at Thaneerpalli [a branch of Shantivanam] they keep merely *om* in brass in their ashram and not even a cross. Likewise, I also object to "crucifying" *om* on the (Roman) cross as they have done in Shantivanam. At Matridham Ashram in Varanasi they keep it just below the crucifix of Jesus and even offer *arati* to it with rest of the images of Jesus and Mary in the ashram. Now it has been removed by the present acharya. In the same way there is a *bhakta's* booklet of *Khrist Chalisa* where *om* is printed on the cover. All these things will misguide others more than help them to understand the message of Jesus Christ in Indian terms.

4   *Om* is not a common platform for our dialogue. We want to assimilate our faith in Christ, remaining culturally and socially as Hindus. In this, we can only use those religious symbols which have more cultural meaning than religious, like decorating the house with *rangoli [kolam]*, lighting oil lamps instead of candles, using saffron dress for *sanyasis*, etc. But however we try, we cannot give a theological interpretation to such a symbol as *om*. If our aim is only to use it to exploit the religious sentiment of the Hindus, then it is wrong in every way.

5   At the same time, I have no objection for using it in our *bhajans*. As a mystic symbol we can use it in *bhajans* and *namavalis* like, *om namah khristaya* [*om*, we bow to Christ], etc. Likewise, we can use it while we use some Upanishadic prayers as well as in ending our own prayers, as in *om shanti! shanti! shanti*! [*om* peace! peace! peace!]

Appendix C

Indianness: What is Wrong?

"Don't think or talk much about culture. God is above culture and you cannot limit God's hand in the name of culture" is another of the comments that I usually receive. After saying this, they generally start to list out all the short comings in our country—caste, untouchability, bribery, corrupt politics, laziness, etc.

"We Indians are like this and we will never grow. See the Western countries. What kind of progress they have made" etc., etc., are their further comments. While quoting several case studies for their arguments, they will naturally forget that they too are part of such a system. But the real tragedy in it is that, while glorifying the Western countries and their concept of "work orientedness" they are still glorifying the past rule of the British both directly and indirectly. This hurts a true son of this soil.

No culture is perfect and no country is perfect. While denying their cultural heritage and tradition, they imagine that either they are living in some no–man's land or creating some kind of "Christian culture" making a cocktail of the "best from Western civilization."

This small paper is not to glorify India, but to bring out some sober truths, which though known to all, are not readily recognized by all. I am thankful to God I was born in this country—with such a rich cultural heritage, which taught a basic human touch to all the endeavors in our life. Just one example, my father was a rich business man, but he became a pauper one fine morning because of bank insolvency. At that time, my mother's father requested my mother to go and live with him with her four children, till her husband recovered. Conversely, mother's reply to him was, "Where Rama is, that is Ayodhya to Sita. If I enjoyed all the pleasure of his wealth so far, let me share in his sufferings also." This is the cultural heritage of India. Note that the purpose of Valmiki in writing *Ramayana* is this, and not for us to fight about Rama.

Of course, now things are changing as we Indians are opting for the leftovers from others' tables even when there is a beautiful feast in our own home. Contextualization is not only coming in Christian ministry but even in the very life of every Indian, for which we are going to pay a heavy price one day. But without knowing the real trouble, some Christians want to fish in the troubled water thinking that their form of "Westernized" Churchianity will quickly yield results to increase their "Church Kingdom." And they liberally criticize everything and anything Indian and glorify the West just for its name –sake.

Though we have several shortcomings as Indians, I have yet to find one perfect nation. I thank God for the gift of being born in India, with all our cultural heritage. A true *bhakta* of Christ finds his own culture and tradition (particularly that of our country) really adding richness to his understanding of his spirituality in the Lord.

References Cited

Aleaz, K. P.
1996 Christian Thought Through Advaita Vedanta. Delhi: ISPCK.

Alexander, E. S.
1994 The Attitudes of British Protestant Missionaries Towards Nationalism in India with Special Reference to Madras Presidency, 1919-1927. New Delhi: Konark Publishers.

Allen, Roland
1962 The Spontaneous Expansion of the Church and the Causes which Hinder It. Grand Rapids: William B. Eerdmanns.

Andrews, C. F.
1912 The Renaissance in India: Its Missionary Aspect. London: United Council for Missionary Education.

Baago, Kaj
1969 Pioneers of Indigenous Christianity. Madras: Christian Literature Society.

Banerjea, K. M.
1975 The Arian Witness. Calcutta: Thacker, Spink and Co.

Barber, B. R.
1912 Kali Charan Banurji: Brahmin, Christian, Saint. Madras: Christian Literature Society for India.

Barrett, David B.
1988 World Christian Encyclopedia. Oxford: Oxford University Press.

Bharati, Dayanand
1992 "A Review Article: Catholic Ashrams: Adopting and Adapting Hindu Dharma." In To All Men All Things. Vol. 2, no. 2, pp. 4-6.
1994 "The Menace of Full Time Ministry." In To All Men All Things. Vol. 4, no. 3, pp. 7-9.

Boyd, Robin
1979 An Introduction to Indian Christian Theology. Madras: The Christian Literature Society.

Bruce, F. F.
1978 "Acts of the Apostles." In Guthrie, D. and Motyer, J. A. (eds.), New Bible Commentary. Third Edition. Leister, England: Inter-Varsity Press.

Chenchiah, P.
1951 "On the Propriety of Christian Women Wearing the Red Dot." In The Guardian, pg. 429.

Clooney, Francis X.
1993 Theology after Vedanta: An Experiment in Comparative Theology. Albany: State University of New York Press. Committee on Black Anglican Concerns
1991 Seed of Hope: Report of a Survey on Combating Racism in the Dioceses of the Church of England. London: The General Synod of the Church of England.

Datta, S. K.
1908 The Desire of India. London: Student Volunteer Missionary Union.

Davis, J. Merle
1949 "Missionary Strategy and the Local Church." International Review of Missions. Vol. 38.

Edgerton, Franklin
1996[1944] The Bhagavad Gita Translated and Interpreted. Delhi: Motilal Banarsidass.

Fakirbhai, Dhanjibhai
n.d. Sri Khrist Gita: Song of the Lord Christ. Bromley, England: The Pilot Book Company.

Fallon, P.
1997 "God in Hinduism: Brahman, Paramatman, Isvara and Bhagavan." In de Smet and Neuner (eds.), Religious Hinduism. Fourth Revised Edition. Bombay: St. Paul's.

Fox, Richard G.
1996 "Communalism and Modernity." In Ludden, David (ed) Making India Hindu: Religion, Community, and the Politics of Democracy in India. New Delhi: Oxford University Press.

Goel, Sita Ram
1988 Catholic Ashrams: Adopting and Adapting Hindu Dharma. New Delhi: Voice of Truth.

Goswami, C. L.
1982 Srimad Bhagavata Mahapurana. Second edition. Gorakhpur: Gita Press.

Goyandka, Janadayal (tr.)
1986 Srimad Bhagawadgita. Gorakhpur: Gita Press.

Griffiths, Michael
1970 Give Up Your Small Ambitions. London: Inter-Varsity Press.

Harshananda, Swami
1996 The Purusasukta: An Exegesis. Bangalore: Ramakrishna Math.

Hedlund, R. E.
1981 Roots of the Great Debate in Mission. Madras: Evangelical Literature Service.

Hesselgrave, David J.
1988 Today's Choices for Tomorrow's Mission: An Evangelical Perspective on Trends and Issues in Mission. Academie Books. Grand Rapids: Zondervan Publishing House.

Hoefer, Herbert E.
2001 Churchless Christianity. Pasadena: William Carey Library.

Hume, R. E.
1985[1931] The Thirteen Principal Upanishads. Second edition, revised. New Delhi: Oxford University Press.

Immanuel, Rajappan D.
1950 The Influence of Hinduism on Indian Christians. Jabalpur: Leonard Theological College.

Jaffrelot, Christopher
1999[1993] The Hindu Nationalist Movement and Indian Politics, 1925 to the 1990s. New Delhi: Penguin Books.

Jauncey, James H.
1965 –Above Ourselves: The True Art of Happiness. Grand Rapids: Zondervan.

Kane, P. V.
1930-1962 History of Dharmasastra. Pune: Bhandarkar Oriental ResearchInstitute.
1997 "Tilaka Mark." In S.G. Moghe (ed), Professor Kane's Contribution to Dharmasastra Literature. New Delhi: D.K. Printworld.

Keller, Carl
1956 "The Vedanta Philosophy and the Message of Christ." In International Review of Missions. Vol. 45, pp. 377-389.

Kelly, J. N. D.
1960 Early Christian Doctrines. Second Edition. New York: Harper & Row.

Khan, Ansar Hussain
1995 The Rediscovery of India: A New Subcontinent. Hyderabad: Orient Longman.

Klostermaier, Klaus K.
1984 Mythologies and Philosophies of Salvation in the Theistic Traditions of India. Ontario: Wilfred Laurier University Press.
1986 Indian Theology In Dialogue. Madras: Christian Literature Society.

Kopf, David
1969 British Orientalism and the Bengal Renaissance. Berkeley: University of California Press.

Lindbeck, George
1984 The Nature of Doctrine: Religion and Theology in a Postliberal Age. Philadelphia: The Westminster Press.

Lipner, Julius J.
1994 Hindus: Their Religious Beliefs and Practices. London: Routledge.
1999 Brahmabandhab Upadhyay: The Life and Thought of a Revolutionary. New Delhi: Oxford University Press.

Lloyd-Jones, D. M.
1966 Studies In The Sermon On The Mount. London: Inter-Varsity Fellowship.

Ludden, David
1996 Making India Hindu: Religion, Community, and the Politics of Democracy in India. New Delhi: Oxford University Press.

Mangalwadi, Vishal
1996 Missionary Conspiracy: Letters to a Postmodern Hindu. Mussoorie: Nivedit Good Books.
1997 India: The Grand Experiment, Surrey, England: Pippa Rann Books.

Mare, Harold W.
1995 "1 Corinthians." In The Study Bible: New International Version. Kenneth Barker (general editor). Grand Rapids: Zondervan Corporation.

Marshall, I. Howard
1983 The Acts of the Apostles. Tyndale New Testament Commentaries. London: Inter-Varsity Press.

Martin, Paul
1996 Missionary of the Indian Road: The Theology of Stanley Jones. Bangalore: Theological Book Trust.

Mishra, Prabhu Datt
1958 "Sermon On The Mount In Verse." (Parvatiiya Pravachan.)

Myers, Kenneth A.
1992 "A Better Way: Proclamation Instead of Protest." In Michael Scott Horton (ed), Power Religion: The Selling Out Of The Evangelical Church? Chicago: Moody Press.

Newbigin, L.
1966 Honest Religion for Secular Man. Lucknow: Lucknow Publishing House.

O'Flaherty, Wendy Doniger
1976 The Origins of Evil in Hindu Mythology. Los Angeles: University of California Press.
1983 Karma and Rebirth in Classical Indian Traditions. Delhi: Motilal Banarsidass.

Olson, Bruce
1995 Bruchko. Lake Mary, FL: Creation House.

Padinjarekara, Joseph
1991 Christ in Ancient Vedas. Burlington, Canada: Welch Publishing Company.

Panikkar, Raimundo
1981 The Unknown Christ of Hinduism. London: Darton, Longman & Todd.
1995 A Dwelling Place for Wisdom. Delhi: Motilal Banarsidass.

Parekh, Manilal C.
1943 Christian Proselytism in India: A Great and Growing Menace. Rajkot, Gujarat: Sri Bhagavata Dharma Mission.

Peter, S. K.
n.d. Nayaa Kaavya. A version of the four gospels in Hindi verse. Delhi: ISPCK.

Pope, G. U.
1900 The Tiruvacagam. Oxford: Oxford University Press.

Prasad, Ishwar
1993 "Inter-Religious Dialogue and Ashrams" In Vandana Mataji (ed), Christian Ashrams: A Movement with a Future? Delhi: ISPCK.

S. Radhakrishnan, S.
1992 The Principal Upanishads. New Delhi: Oxford University Press.

1940 Eastern Religions and Western Thought. London: Oxford University Press.

Sauliere, A. and S. Rajamanickam
1995 His Star in the East. Anand, Gujarat: Gujarat Sahitya Prakash.

Rambachan, Anantanand
1995 The Limits of Scripture: Vivekananda's Reinterpretation of the Vedas. Delhi: Sri Satguru Publications.

Rangarajan, V.
1979 "Vedanta Embraces Christianity." In Christianity in India: A Critical Study. Madras: Vivekananda Kendra.

Raychaudhuri, Tapan
1999 Perceptions, Emotions, Sensibilities: Essays on India's Colonial and Post-Colonial Experiences. New Delhi: Oxford University Press.

Richard, H. L.
1993-4 "The Arian Witness Recalled: Vedic Sacrifice and Fulfillment Theology." In To All Men All Things. Vol. 3, no. 3, pp. 1-7 and vol. 4 no. 1, pp. 1-5.
2000 "Rethinking Community." In Dharma Deepika, July 2000, pp 51-58.

Richard, H. L. (ed.)
1995 R. C. Das: Evangelical Prophet for Contextual Christianity. Delhi: ISPCK.

Rokhaya, R. B.
1996 "What if all Nepalis became Christians?" In Face to Face. Number 9.

Ryrie, C. Caldwell
1978 Ryrie Study Bible. Chicago: Moody Press.

Sanders, Oswald
1994 Spiritual Leadership. Chicago: Moody Press.

Schmidt, Robert
1999 The Transformation of the Church. Oregon: Transformation Media.

Selvanayagam, Israel
1996 The Dynamics of Hindu Traditions. Bangalore: Asian Trading Corporation.

Shaw, Ellis O.
1986 Rural Hinduism: Some Observations and Experiences. Madras: Christian Literature Society.

Shourie, Arun
1994 Missionaries in India: Continuities, Changes, Dilemmas. New Delhi: ASA Publications.

Smet, Richard V. de
1972 "The Gita in Time and Beyond Time." In The Bhagavad Gita and the Bible. New Delhi: Unity Books.

Staffner, Hans
1987 Jesus Christ and The Hindu Community. Anand, Gujarat: Gujarat Sahitya Prakash.

Stietencron, Heinrich von
1991 "Hinduism: On the Proper Use of a Deceptive Term." In Sontheimer, Gunther D. and Kulke, Hermann (eds), Hinduism Reconsidered. Delhi: Manohar Books.

Stott, John
1970 Christ the Controversialist. Downers Grove, IL: Inter-Varsity Press.
1989 Issues Facing Christians Today. Bombay: Gospel Literature Service.

Sundarraj, Ebenezer
1985 "Caste and Church." In India Church Growth Quarterly. Vol. 7, no. 2, pp. 81-84.

Thangasamy, D. A. (ed.)
1966 The Theology of Chenchiah. Confessing the Faith in India. Calcutta: YMCA for the Christian Institute for the Study of Religion and Society.

Thannickal, John Samuel
1975 Ashram: A Communicating Community. A dissertation presented to the faculty of The School of World Mission and Institute of Church Growth, Fuller Theological Seminary.

Tharoor, Shashi
1994 The Great Indian Novel. Delhi: Picador.

Thomas, M. M.
1969 The Acknowledged Christ of the Indian Renaissance. London: SCM Press.

Tilak, B. G.
1986[1935] Srimad Bhagavadgita-Rahasya. 7th Edition. Pune: Tilak Brothers.

Titus, D.P.
1982 Fulfillment of the Vedic Quest in the Lord Jesus Christ. Privately published in India.
1989 St. John's Gospel: It's Witness to India. Privately published in India.
1993 The Concept of Divine Sacrifice in the Bible and Vedic Scriptures. Privately published in India.

Vempeny, Ishanand
1988 Krsna And Christ. Anand, Gujarat: Gujarat Sahitya Prakash.

Vivekananda, Swami
1986 Selections from the Complete Works of Swami Vivekananda. Calcutta: Advaita Ashram.

Wald, S. N.
1962 "Christian Terminology in Hindi." In Missionstudien 1.

Whaling, Frank
1966 An Approach to Dialogue with Hinduism. Lucknow: Lucknow Publishing House.

Wheaton, David H.
1978 "1 Peter." In Guthrie, D. and Motyer, J. A. (eds.), New Bible Commentary. Third Edition. Leister, England: Inter-Varsity Press.

Wilkins, W. J.
1991[1900] Hindu Mythology: Vedic & Puranic. 2nd edition. New Delhi: Heritage Publishers.

Wright, Christopher J. H.
1983 Living as the People of God: The Relevance of O.T. Ethics. London: Inter-Varsity Press.

Yesudasan, Savarirayan
1940[1931] Daivabhaktiyam Desabhaktiyam. (Tamil.) Tirupathur, India: Christukula Ashram.

Zupanov, Ines G.
1999 Disputed Mission. New Delhi: Oxford University Press.

Scriptural References Cited

INDEX OF NAMES

SUBJECT INDEX